Smudging

The Ultimate Guide to Spiritual Cleansing, Psychic Protection, and Energy Clearing

© Copyright 2024 - All rights reserved.

The content contained within this book may not be reproduced, duplicated, or transmitted without direct written permission from the author or the publisher.

Under no circumstances will any blame or legal responsibility be held against the publisher, or author, for any damages, reparation, or monetary loss due to the information contained within this book, either directly or indirectly.

Legal Notice:

This book is copyright protected. It is only for personal use. You cannot amend, distribute, sell, use, quote, or paraphrase any part of the content within this book without the consent of the author or publisher.

Disclaimer Notice:

Please note the information contained within this document is for educational and entertainment purposes only. All effort has been executed to present accurate, up-to-date, reliable, and complete information. No warranties of any kind are declared or implied. Readers acknowledge that the author is not engaging in the rendering of legal, financial, medical, or professional advice. The content within this book has been derived from various sources. Please consult a licensed professional before attempting any techniques outlined in this book.

By reading this document, the reader agrees that under no circumstances is the author responsible for any losses, direct or indirect, that are incurred as a result of the use of the information contained within this document, including, but not limited to, errors, omissions, or inaccuracies.

Your Free Gift
(only available for a limited time)

Thanks for getting this book! If you want to learn more about various spirituality topics, then join Mari Silva's community and get a free guided meditation MP3 for awakening your third eye. This guided meditation mp3 is designed to open and strengthen ones third eye so you can experience a higher state of consciousness. Simply visit the link below the image to get started.

https://spiritualityspot.com/meditation

Or, Scan the QR code!

Table of Contents

INTRODUCTION 1
CHAPTER 1: THE POWER OF SMUDGING 3
CHAPTER 2: IDENTIFYING NEGATIVE ENERGY 13
CHAPTER 3: BEFORE YOU START 23
CHAPTER 4: HERBS, RESINS, AND OILS 32
CHAPTER 5: HOW TO SMUDGE 46
CHAPTER 6: SMUDGING ALTERNATIVES 57
CHAPTER 7: CRAFTING YOUR SUPPLIES 67
CHAPTER 8: PSYCHIC PROTECTION METHODS 75
CHAPTER 9: CRYSTALS AND SMUDGING 86
CHAPTER 10: HEALING WITH SMUDGING 99
CONCLUSION 108
HERE'S ANOTHER BOOK BY MARI SILVA THAT YOU MIGHT LIKE 110
YOUR FREE GIFT (ONLY AVAILABLE FOR A LIMITED TIME) 111
REFERENCES 112

Introduction

When someone mentions "smudging your home," what thoughts come to mind? Do you feel a bit intimidated? Maybe it sounds complicated, messy, or weird. Even though smudging has gained popularity in recent years, many people still feel overwhelmed by the idea of smudging their homes. It's understandable to be skeptical or unsure, thinking it may involve a lot of smoke and strange religious rituals. Some may even find the whole process too complex. Sometimes, even with the intention and enthusiasm to smudge, people give up at the first hurdle — finding a smudge stick to buy!

Like anything new, it's helpful to understand the benefits of the process you're considering. Why should you smudge your home? Is it actually necessary? Can you make it simple and enjoyable? Are there alternative ways to clear the energy in your home? And what makes smudging so special? Think of a ritual like dating, for example. The more questions you ask, the sooner you'll know if it's worth investing in this relationship. The word "relationship" is used in the sense that entering the world of smudging ideally means entering a beautiful, long-term connection. Like any relationship, you'll have to go through many stages to reach a place of deep intimacy and commitment.

In this book, you'll get the answer to all of your questions and learn various ways to smudge, including some very simple techniques you can enjoy more than once a day. The energy in your home can shift after a long day, bringing along busy, hectic, and sometimes negative energies from outside. In such situations, a quick two-to-three-minute smudging session can work wonders to calm and purify the space and cleanse your energy. The beauty of smudging is that it can be as simple and quick or as elaborate and intricate as you want. Once you grasp the basics and explore optional add-ons, you'll feel more empowered to create your own rituals which suit your situation.

Smudging can be an easy, centering, enjoyable, and grounding experience. However, you'll notice, above all else, the ability to purify energy in your space. By the time you have finished reading this book, you'll feel confident, empowered, and ready to take charge of the energy in your home—and your life—through smudging. You'll be excited and enthusiastic about creating a whole new level of positive energy in your own space.

Chapter 1: The Power of Smudging

Smudging purifies the energy of the object or person in focus.
https://unsplash.com/photos/0-c1F9uukx8

Smudging is an ancient form of cleansing used on a person, an object, or a space using the smoke of burning herbs. The herbs can be any of the following; dried sage, sweetgrass, lavender, cedar, rosemary, and other plants with beneficial properties. Smudging (or smoke cleansing) purifies the energy of the object or person in focus. Since ancient times, different cultures have had their own unique traditions for smudging. These traditions often involved prayers, meditations, or other rituals. For example, in some Native American cultures, sweetgrass is burned during an elaborate ceremony meant to release the positive energy of the sacred plant into the air. Whatever your reason for wanting to spiritually cleanse an area, object, or person, this chapter will introduce you to the practice of smudging, explore its background, explain how it works, and explore its benefits.

How Does Smudging Work?

The practice of smudging is relatively simple; it only has a few fundamental tenets:

- Smudging relies on setting an intention. For example, you form an intention to cleanse your space of negative energy or invite positive energy into your home.
- Once your intention is set, light the herb and allow it to become engulfed in flames until it begins to smoke. Always do this, bearing in mind safety factors. Then, waft the smoke around a person's body, a space, or an object with your hand or using a feather. If purifying the body, start at the feet and move up to the head.
- When purging a space or an object, windows must be open, or you can perform the ritual outdoors.
- During cleansing, imagine the manifestation of your intention – you see the negative energy leaving you and positive vibes surrounding you, the object, or the space in question.
- Once you have cleansed yourself, the object, or your space, you should extinguish the herb safely and thank it for its service.
- Some practitioners love to finish their smudging ritual with a closing prayer or mantra. You can recite this when you feel negativity around yourself, the person or object you wanted to purify has left, or when you've finished cleansing a space.

- Whether you perform the closing part or not, it's recommended that you repeat your intention before closing the ceremony.
- The absence of negativity and positive changes in the person, object, or environment are indicators of smudging's effectiveness.
- The frequency of smudging depends on the practice – it can be done annually, during festivities, or as frequently as you feel the need to ward off negativity.

Smudging in Different Cultures

Smudging -or burning herbs to purify the energy of a space – has enjoyed a resurgence of popularity in recent years as more and more people are exploring alternative lifestyles. Its origins are in ancient civilizations and have long been associated with Native American and Indigenous cultures. In Native American cultures, the smudging ritual involves using a bundle of sage, sweetgrass, cedar, tobacco, or other herbs that have been dried and bound together into a slow-burning purification tool. Sometimes entire leaves or branches are placed in a fireproof container and lit until they begin smoking, and the smoke is then used to cleanse the area or person of negative energy. A person who smoke-cleanses one or more people can lead the ritual instead of depending on a regular practitioner. They either blow the smoke out toward the recipient or space, or the recipient inhales the smoke. According to Native American beliefs, inhaled herbal smoke heals a person's entire being. When the plants burn down, their ashes are returned to their origin – usually by scattering them on the bare ground. It is believed that ashes absorb negative energy, so discarding them helps you to dispose of that negativity. Smudging is also used during prayer or meditation and for connecting with the spirit world.

Native Americans have different beliefs regarding the benefits of each herb used for smudging. For example, they praise sweetgrass for drawing in positive vibes and cedar for facilitating blessings and cleansing the body from disease. Sage, which they believe can ward off any form of negativity, has a unique origin story. According to a Native American legend, the herb sage first appeared a very long time ago when a village was full of negativity. Everyone felt bad about themselves and others, and everything seemed to be going wrong for everyone. One day, a young man showed up carrying a bundle of herbs in his arms. He introduced the herb to the villagers as sage, a plant that can empower anyone to handle negativity. He built a fire, lit the sage, and showed the villagers how to smudge themselves. The villagers started to feel good about themselves and began to experience success in their endeavors. The young man disappeared, but the villagers noticed that sage had begun to grow in their area. So, they started using it regularly for cleansing.

For centuries, Shamans have believed that smudging is a powerful way to clear negative energy and create a sense of balance and harmony in any space. As the smoke travels through the air, it is believed to have the power to cleanse a space of negative energies while creating positive feelings and raising vibrations. In shamanic traditions, smudging involves a prayer or ritual, after which the smoke is sent into the four cardinal directions. Besides this, different practitioners and tribes have diversified methods and techniques for smudging, including when and how it's used. Shamans readily use smudging for divination and cleansing when preparing for a rite or ceremony. Modern practitioners also use it to restore emotional, physical, and mental balance, ward off negativity, and enhance their shamanic practices. They also smudge their magical tools and sacred spaces - often before and after use - to restore balance. Some even smoke-cleanse themselves daily to maintain a centered state of being, which enables them to reach a trance-like state for their meditative practices.

Native Americans and Shamans also recommended smudging when someone had been in contact with a sick person (physically or mentally), emotionally unbalanced individuals, or those who had been otherwise affected by negative influences.

Benefits of Smudging

As you'll see in the text below, smudging has numerous benefits for your physical, mental, spiritual, and emotional well-being.

Spiritual

One of the fundamental benefits of smudging is its spiritual aspect. This stems from the belief that when practiced in sacred ceremonies, smoke cleansing sends away any built-up negative energy and attracts positive intentions from nature, allowing you to manifest your desires more easily. It isn't used to obtain spiritual awareness and connection to one's higher self in many Native and Indigenous cultures for no reason!

Moreover, by focusing on each individual herb during your ritual, you will be able to connect with its medicinal properties and obtain powerful healing agents for physical, emotional, and mental health issues. Once you reach the healing stage, you'll be even more empowered to ward off stress-inducing negative vibes.

Smudging can help you heal from negative influences from past traumas, malicious people in your environment, or bad experiences in any aspect of your life. Your sense of smell is linked to instinct and memory recall functions, which is another reason the aroma of smudged herbs can help you work through stress and traumatic events. As you inhale their soothing scent, the herbs will help you allay the fear, anger, anxiety, grief, and triggers you associate with past traumas.

Restoring your energetic balance after these events fosters a positive attitude for meditation and spiritual rituals. Not only that, but certain herbs contain bioactive compounds that, when inhaled, improve intention-setting abilities and insight. Whether you use it for spiritual practices or self-improvement, clearing out negativity from and around you will benefit your spiritual well-being.

Certain herbs are blessed with protective abilities. Smudging them can help you ward off evil forces and psychic attacks during spiritual work. They help chase away negative thoughts triggered by outside influences and create a shield around you to repel similar intrusions in the future. The protective effects of smudging can also come in handy when dealing with difficult people or preparing to handle particularly challenging situations.

Smudging enhances creativity in all aspects of life. Whatever problem you're trying to solve, purifying yourself with cleansing smoke will help you find innovative solutions. It can boost your productivity by inspiring you with new ideas. If you're an artist experiencing a creative block, the herbs can reveal new pathways for your creative juices to flow.

The cleansing and purifying properties of herbs burned while smudging can open up intuition, encouraging you to start trusting your gut feelings. If you feel like your judgment is clouded and this is blocking your intuition, practicing smudging could enable your inner psychic senses to reveal themselves. By becoming familiar with your psychic gifts, you sharpen your intuition and keep it clear of judgmental or biased ideas and beliefs.

Lastly, smudging is good for spiritual practices because it encourages self-love. After all, there is no better way to begin exploring and working on your spirituality than by accepting yourself. Some believe this benefit comes from the burned herbs' ability to open and unblock chakras associated with self-love and acceptance.

Psychological

One of the most outstanding benefits of smoke cleansing is its ability to help reduce stress and anxiety levels. This can be achieved through the calming effects of the herbs' aromas. Burning herbs like sage or cedar releases a pleasant aroma that promotes calmness and relaxation in the body and mind.

Certain herbs contain phytochemicals that stimulate anti-excitatory receptors and neurotransmitters in the brain, effectively relieving anxiety symptoms. Because of their ability to chase away harmful feelings, smudging can uplift your mood quickly. Regularly cleansing with sage could help you manage your symptoms if you suffer from depression or other mood-related conditions.

Energetic

Smudging promotes a sense of clarity, boosts the sensation of calmness and peace, improves your energy levels, and fosters self-awareness. This smudging benefit stems from the herbs' ability to encourage mindful presence during rituals. The energetic influence of the herbs used in smudging enables you to actively engage with all five senses. By empowering you energetically, certain burned herbs can also foster clear thinking and quick reactions, making it easier for you to pick up spiritual signals through your senses. If boosting your mood doesn't make you consider trying your hand at smudging, the possibility of improved clarity and awareness certainly will.

When you feel more energized, your mind is sharp, enabling you to think more positively and develop helpful and productive thought patterns. This proves that positive energy has a higher vibrational frequency. Besides making you feel good physically, emotionally, and mentally, smudging will also improve your cognitive function. This could help you combat the effects of neurodegenerative conditions like Alzheimer's disease and dementia. The reason for this lies in the effect of smoked herbs on your hormones. Many mental and neurodegenerative conditions develop due to adrenal fatigue – a state caused by hormonal misbalance of the adrenal glands, which occurs during stress. In a similar vein, healthy people's loss of neurons can also result in stress-induced fatigue. As a result, you may suffer from cognitive impairments, even if you don't have a neurodegenerative or mental health condition. This often happens due to inflammatory conditions in the body, which inevitably affect the nervous system. Whether accompanied by anxiety, impaired cognitive functions, or any other symptoms, conditions affecting cognitive and mental health can make the sufferer feel that relief is impossible to achieve. The energizing effect of smudging can chase away these negative thoughts, empowering the person to find efficient solutions and, more importantly, relief for their symptoms. The two most important hormones released by the adrenal glands, norepinephrine and epinephrine, must be in balance to achieve this. Cortisol, serotonin, and dopamine – more hormones responsible for controlling energy levels – are also positively affected by smudging. The smoke of certain herbs restores the optimal timing for the release of these chemicals.

Certain herbs have a proven beneficial effect on your chakra system – the complex entity representing your energy. The chakra system has seven main access points, known as chakras. The chakras are responsible for the healthy flow of energy through your body. If any of them is blocked or not working properly, this affects your entire energy system. Smudging herbs associated with the individual chakras (or all of your chakras) can help clear them out. As you unblock your energy centers, you cleanse, shield, and re-energize your mind, body, and soul. For example, rosemary can open up your heart chakra, enabling you to develop (self) compassion and understanding. Likewise, the same herb can unblock your third eye chakra, the energy center responsible for spiritual clarity and psychic awareness.

Physical

Another way smudging can boost your energy is by improving the quality of your sleep. Negative energy influences often leave you with sleepless nights. Or, even if you manage to sleep for a few hours, you feel more tired after waking up than before going to bed. Smudging before sleep can ward off any negative energies hindering your sleep, allowing you to feel energized and productive throughout the following day. It will help you fall asleep faster and grant you uninterrupted sleep – and if you do wake up during the night, you'll fall back asleep instead of being plagued by worries about the coming day.

Beyond normalizing your sleep patterns, smoke from smudging can also help improve your skin and boost the function of many organs and organ systems, including the respiratory, gastrointestinal, and circulatory systems. The air-purifying effects of the smoke mean that your skin will be exposed to fewer pollutants, allowing it to heal and regenerate. Due to its sleep-and energy-boosting benefits, smudging will make your skin look positively radiant and rejuvenated. Likewise, pure air will improve your lung function and combat the symptoms of chronic and acute respiratory conditions.

Certain herbs have analgesic properties, meaning they can bring relief to headaches, heartburn, muscle aches, and joint pains. The anti-inflammatory compounds in herbs like sage, rosemary, and others further emphasize this benefit.

Some herbs can also boost immune function, helping you to ward off infections and combat existing ones. They foster immune cell production and improve the function of all body parts responsible for healthy immunity, including the bone marrow, spleen, thymus, gut, and skin.

Moreover, the soothing effects of smudged herbs can lower your heart rate and blood pressure, positively contributing to your heart health. When feeling anxious or stressed, inhaling herbal smoke regulates your breathing pattern, allowing you to take more oxygen into your body. This further enhances the healing effects of smudging, as oxygen is needed for neutralizing free radicals – the byproducts of oxidative stress and the precursors of many physical and mental health conditions.

Environmental

Smoke cleansing has also been proven to have antiseptic properties. In other words, the smoke from the herbs can effectively purify the air in any room containing viruses, fungi, or bacteria that can cause common respiratory issues or illnesses like asthma, colds, and flu. Besides the aforementioned microorganisms and their byproducts, herbs used in smudging can eliminate potential allergens like dust, pollen, mold spores, and pet dander – relieving those insufferable allergy symptoms. This is why smoke cleansing is ideal for disinfecting indoor spaces without using harmful chemicals or sprays.

Cleaner air is known for improved oxygen concentration levels, making the atmosphere perfect for studying or working on assignments requiring intense focus and a wider attention span. Certain herbs, like sage, are also known for their insect-repellent abilities. Let's face it, who wouldn't want to take advantage of this during the summer when mosquitos make life impossible?

Due to the pleasantly calming aroma of the burned herbs, smudging can also be seen as a form of aromatherapy. Inhaling soothing herbal fragrances foster neurotransmitter modulation in the brain. Neurotransmitters are chemicals needed to transport and process information throughout the nervous system. In other words, smudging enables your nervous system to intake, process, and transmit information more effectively.

Another reason smudging with certain herbs purifies space is that the smoke neutralizes *positive ions* (not to be confused with positive vibes, which are also beneficial). Positive ions are particles that tie down energy, making it unavailable for harnessing or manipulation. You foster positive ion accumulation in the air when you're angry or stressed. It starts with the positively charged air you release from your lungs, which permeates the energy in the room. Then, the room's air becomes stagnant due to the prevailing number of positive ions. After a while, you start feeling lethargic and can't seem to embrace positivity no matter how hard you try. Herbs used in smoke cleansing can make negative ions from positive ones, effectively purging the atmosphere from the latter.

The space-cleansing benefits of smudging can come in handy when moving into a new home or when negativity has been a long-term inhabitant of your home or office. For example, if you had an abusive or disruptive relationship with a difficult person you lived with – and they've moved out of your shared space – smudging the property could ensure all the negativity they invited into it leaves too.

Smoke cleansing can also be an efficient way to purify objects. If you work with magical or spiritual tools, regularly smudging them can significantly enhance their power and effectiveness. Even cleaning everyday objects has beneficial effects on the energetic makeup of their environment. This is particularly true for antique items, which have probably accumulated a plethora of different energies during their lifetime. Simply passing a lit smudge stick over them will ensure their aura can't negatively affect you, your space, or those around you.

Another superb idea for smudging objects is using herbal smoke on presents you intend to give. By infusing your gifts with a soothing aroma of herbs, you're passing on their benefits to the recipients, allowing them to fill their space and person with positivity.

Ethical Considerations Regarding the Practice of Smudging

Modern spiritual and new-age shamanic practitioners often boast about smudging being a closed practice, indicating that its best used by those who understand its cultural origins. While acting contrary to this would imply that the practice has become an example of cultural appropriation (when one culture takes elements from another without permission or understanding the original context), there is much more to this topic. Nevertheless, to use smudging respectfully, you must approach the practice with greater sensitivity, respect, and understanding.

More and more non-Natives (including influential celebrities) are showcasing the use of this practice for their own spiritual explorations without fully understanding its history and cultural significance. Smoke cleansing can be seen as inappropriate if done without courteous respect for the tradition. That being said, it's crucial to note that not everyone practices smudging this way out of disrespect. They simply see its spiritual benefit. However, even if you have the best intentions, you can cause harm if you don't properly respect the traditions surrounding the practice. When engaging in smudging, it's fundamental to take time to research its history and understand its significance within the original contexts. Doing this helps prevent the practice from becoming cultural appropriation.

Cultural appropriation often entails adopting symbols from other cultures or attempting to pass off traditional practices as your own. This happens because many people learn about smudging from non-research-based books, TV shows, and movies rather than obtaining information from traditional sources. Consequently, they fail to gain knowledge of its spiritual significance and implications.

Another factor to consider is the respectful use of sacred plants and responsible material sourcing. These are both critical to promote sustainable and responsible use of herbs and to honor the cultural and spiritual traditions of Indigenous and Native American communities. The best way to source your material ethically is to use herbs growing in your area. Find out what plants grow near you and the benefits they can provide for spiritual cleansing.

Chapter 2: Identifying Negative Energy

Smudging is about driving away the negative energy from a space or living being – and making space for positive energy to enter.
https://www.pexels.com/photo/man-falling-carton-boxes-with-negative-words-7203956/

As you may have realized by now, smudging is all about driving away the negative energy from a place or a living being, making space for positive energy to enter. But before you can do that, you need to be certain that the energy contained in the object is negative. How can you point out that someone or something is surrounded by negative energy? It is easy to make the identification once you get the hang of the process. To make understanding the intriguing specifics of the method easier still, here are the fundamentals of sensing and recognizing energy itself.

What Is Energy?

In physics, energy is nothing more than a force that can be exerted to perform work. But the same physics has also given mankind the direct relationship between matter and energy. Remember Albert Einstein's famous equation, $E=mc^2$ ("E" is energy, and "m" stands for mass or matter)? Thus, energy isn't just an abstract, invisible entity that grants force to objects. It is a very real thing that can be felt all around you.

Energy was present before the birth of the universe, and it will remain long after the world is no more. In its raw state, it is pure, powerful, and all-encompassing. It cannot be seen or felt if you don't know what you are looking for. Different forms of energy vibrate at different frequencies. And the most important form of energy is thoughts. They vibrate at different frequencies too.

What Is Energy Vibration and Movement?

The vibration of energy is governed by the Law of Vibration. It states that all forms of energy are constantly vibrating. No energy is ever at rest, for if it is, then it is energy no longer but a void of nothingness, sort of a vacuum. The frequency of vibration determines the kind of energy it is.

Frequencies that are alike tend to resonate with each other, merging together to form a greater kind of that energy. They travel across the universe, continuing to merge with energies that vibrate at their frequency – ever accumulating, ever-growing. This concept is easier to understand with an energy body instead of a physical body.

Energy Body and Its Significance

An energy body (alternatively called an Astral body) is nothing but a physical body as seen in the form of pure energy. It's like looking at your body in a different spectrum, like infrared. It is said that your energy body is around five inches larger than your physical body. It comprises various energy centers (Chakras) and energy channels (Meridians). Chakras ensure the healthy function of your physical body, whereas Meridians are responsible for circulating the absorbed energy throughout the body.

In the energy body, your thoughts are visible fragments of your mind, and you can feel the frequency of their vibration. When you think about something for the first time, a fragment of that thought is generated in your energy body. Your mind sends out the frequency of that thought's vibrations into the universe. But to manifest that thought into something real and visible in the physical sense, you need to establish energetic harmony.

What Is Energetic Harmony?

In simple words, energetic harmony is a balance between different kinds of energy. Take musical harmony, for instance. Just like different notes, tempos, pitches, etc., are played in perfect sync to form a musical harmony, different kinds and frequencies of energy come together to give rise to an energetic harmony.

This fantastic music of the universe can either be profoundly soothing or insanely chaotic. It entirely depends upon the keys that you play to achieve that harmony. These keys are nothing but your thoughts. If you play the right keys (read: think positive thoughts), like thinking about cheering up your neighbors or giving a percentage of your salary to charity, then the vibrations generated will resonate with other similar vibrations in the universe, bringing about an amazingly positive energetic harmony.

On the other hand, if you play the wrong keys (read: think negative thoughts), like feeling jealous of your friend's success or planning revenge on an enemy, then those vibrations will merge only with other similar vibrations, giving rise to a cacophony of negative energetic harmony (read: utter chaos).

That is what negative energy looks and feels like, and it is what will be identified in this chapter. But before getting to the process of identifying that energy, it is important to understand the concept of negative energy in depth.

What Is Negative Energy?

In its raw form, energy is neither positive nor negative. It just is. Your thoughts make the energy lean toward the polar extremes. Bad thoughts will generate negative energy in a space or an individual. It always starts off small. In the initial stages, an infinitesimal part of your surroundings will be converted to negative energy.

This part will attract other similar negative energies from the universe, growing in proportion with the multiple merges until it eventually occupies the entire space, pushing out the neutral and positive energies. That is when smudging comes into the picture to make space for positivity. Neutral energy can be converted to negative from three possible sources.

1. **Negative Self**

    Do you tend to dwell on your regrets rather than thinking about your promising future? Do feelings of jealousy eat you up on the inside? Do you hate people more than you feel love for them? Is your mind often occupied with negative thoughts? If you answered even one of these questions in the affirmative, then you have negative energy within and around you.

    It may simply be a small dark patch in your energy body or a radiating aura of negativity. Either way, your own dark thoughts brought the rancid atmosphere to life.

2. **Negative People**

    It doesn't always have to be you who brings negative energy to your energy body. You don't have to be inherently negative. The energy that the people around you project can also affect your aura. Suppose you let the negativity of your family, friends, and acquaintances influence your thoughts. In that case, your negative energy is merging with theirs and expanding in your surroundings, leaving no place for positivity.

3. **Negative Surroundings**

    When you enter a space rife with negative energy, there is a high chance that it may seep into your positive/neutral energy body. It so happens that, sometimes, when you enter a room, a feeling of discomfort immediately creeps up on you. That is most probably because of the negative energy confined in it. It may start affecting your thoughts, generating gloomy images of the past in your mind.

Negative surroundings like that could turn out to be anything. It could be a place where you have had a bad encounter in the past, like a sports ground where you lost to the opposition. Or it could be a space you associate with negative occurrences, like a morgue.

In essence, negative energy is nothing but a collection of bad thoughts. The greater the number of bad thoughts confined in a space, the more negative energy it will contain. And often, it is not easily recognizable until it's too late - when the negativity entirely consumes your soul. It can be compared to cancer, curable when detected in the early stages but fatal if diagnosed late.

No need to fret, however. Here you will learn everything there is to know about identifying negative energy in its simplest, most infinitesimal forms so that you can detect it early and smudge the place before the negativity spreads out of control.

How to Identify Negative Energy

Now that you know what negative energy is and what it looks and feels like, identifying it won't be much of a problem. You may find it difficult initially, but once you get used to the process, it will become second nature to you. It's like learning how to ride a bike. You may fall a few times at first, but eventually, you will get it right. You just need to keep a lookout for the signs.

What to Look for While Identifying Negative Energy?

The line between right and wrong, good and bad, positive and negative, is sometimes blurred. You can overlook something that is commonly considered to be wrong but may be right for you. These apparently good things may eventually lead to something decidedly bad, like some innocent prank gone wrong. Hence, avoiding the gray areas and focusing on definite negativity while identifying negative energy is better. Here's what you may consider looking for.

- Incessant health problems for you and in the people around you
- Repeated arguments and bad vibes between two or more individuals

- Unsolvable work-related issues that keep piling up
- An overall lack of success
- A general feeling of lethargy
- Blanking out often and at odd times
- A constant feeling of unease and/or anxiety
- Continued lack of sleep, at least for a week
- Unusual occurrences around the place that cannot be rationally explained

As you can see, the only point that isn't inherently negative is the last one. Those unusual occurrences may also lead to something good. But it's always better to be safe than sorry. And anyway, smudging removes only negative energy from a place and keeps the positivity. So, if the rationally inexplicable happenings lead to something positive, their source won't be removed through smudging.

You can identify negative energy using one or all three mediums: the people, yourself, or the environment. Ask the following questions to determine the presence of negative energy.

- **Identification through People**

Is there a general sense of animosity between people? Are they often on edge? Do full-blown arguments break out from the tiniest of disagreements? Are they often down with the flu? Is someone nearly always afflicted with some health issues every second of every day? Has nobody found success in their undertakings despite working hard? Does nobody seem to muster the strength to work hard?

- **Identification through Yourself**

This is probably the easiest way to identify negative energy. After all, you know yourself better than you know others.

Do you often tend to lose focus on the task at hand? Does your mind go blank for long periods (zero-state of thinking)? Do you tend to dwell more on negative thoughts than on positive ones? Are you often sick with various kinds of health problems, one after the other, like fever one week followed by constipation the next, and so on? Do you suffer from the same health issue far longer than usual?

Is your mind occupied with positive or negative thoughts while trying to sleep? Are you often so critical of something that you tend to lose sight of its virtue? Do you find yourself complaining about the smallest of things? Do you overthink and overanalyze your mistakes instead of focusing on the good parts or solutions?

- **Identification through the Environment**

This is more of a comparative method than an identification medium in itself. Simply ask yourself the above questions in different environments. For instance, is your mind occupied with negative thoughts at home? Then go to your friend's place and see if those negative thoughts still haunt you. If they don't, then it's likely that the negative energy exists in your home. But if they do follow you, then there is a high probability that the negative energy lies within you.

Alternatively, are your colleagues in a constant state of agitation at your workplace? But do they seem happy and content when you go out for drinks? Then the negative energy is present at your workplace. However, if your colleagues are still agitated during the evening out, then it's likely that negative energy is present within the group.

Another way to determine the existence of negative energy in the environment is to go with your instincts or gut feelings. Do you suddenly feel uncomfortable after entering a room? Do goosebumps start creeping up your spine when visiting an unknown place?

Granted, these questions are often hard to answer if you are just starting out on your identification journey, especially the last ones. You may fail to correctly recognize negative energy for what it is initially. But know that it is a process of trial and error. It's perfectly okay if you keep failing at first, but as soon as you can correctly identify the presence of negative energy, you will rarely fail again.

There is another easier way of identifying negative energy, and that is by analyzing emotions. Negative energy produces negative emotions. Thus, you need to watch out for the frequency of the following emotions in yourself or in others around you.

- **Anger**

Do small things make you or others angry? Let's say that you're getting ready to go to work, and your younger brother has misplaced your favorite shirt. Is your first instinct to lash out at him instead of calmly asking him about it?

- **Irritation**

Do you often find yourself irritated by the smallest of things? For example, you are trying to get some work done. Suddenly, someone enters your cubicle without knocking. Does that annoy you?

- **Depression**

These days, depression has become one of the most commonly felt negative emotions in the world, so much so that it is categorized as a medical illness. Are you feeling utter hopelessness? Has sadness enveloped your heart? On a happy occasion, do you find yourself brooding in a corner?

- **Fear**

At times, it is okay to feel fear, like arachnophobes feel when they spot a spider, or when you're witnessing/experiencing something horrific, or if you're watching a horror movie. But if you're afraid almost all the time, then that may be the result of negative energy.

- **Anxiety**

Anxiety and fear often go hand in hand. Whenever you're anxious about undertaking a task, you probably fear botching that task. Does something as simple as getting out of bed and going about your day make you anxious? Are you often nervous about doing little things, like talking to your neighbors or watching the news?

- **Guilt**

You feel guilty when you do something that goes against your moral code. And that is usually good because it keeps your behavior in check. But when you start dwelling on that guilt, so much so that it overwhelms you, that is probably due to negative energy.

- **Envy**

Feelings of jealousy are quite common among humans. If someone takes what is yours, rightfully so or otherwise, it is normal to feel a bit of envy. But if you're consumed by that emotion, then it will give rise to other negative emotions. And you will eventually be surrounded by negative energy.

- **Contempt**

There is a very thin line separating pride and contempt. Feeling proud of your accomplishment? Good. But do you look down on those who cannot accomplish what you did? That's contempt, and it is definitely a negative emotion. You may be steeped in negative energy if you often feel contemptuous toward others.

- **Hate**

They say that without hate, there can be no love. But it doesn't mean that you should let hate govern or dictate your actions. Do you tend to hate people without rhyme or reason? Is your first instinct after meeting someone new to hate them? Do even the good actions of your fellow humans generate hatred in your heart?

These are the most common emotions you can easily use to identify negative energy. Many other emotions imply the presence of negative energy, like shame, misery, loneliness, disgust, etc., but people don't usually express these. Even you may not realize your loneliness unless someone points it out!

What NOT to Look for While Identifying Negative Energy

Now that you know the signs to identify negative energy, it is time to learn what to avoid taking that knowledge into consideration. On rare occasions, it is easy to mistake something positive for negative energy. At other times, it is easier still to blame negative energy when you are experiencing the direct consequences of your actions.

- **Fleeting Negativity**

Is it the first time in a while that you were angry at someone? Have your colleagues been arguing only for a while? Did your health problems last no longer than a day or two? These may not be instances of negative energy. When the problems fester and keep piling up over several days, only then could it be a cause for concern.

- **Wrong Action for the Right Reasons**

When you notice someone displaying a negative emotion, try to figure out why they feel that way. It may be that a person is angry because they saw some injustice being done. You may be feeling anxious because you want to get the task done perfectly. Your actions or emotions may be negative, but if your reasons for doing/displaying them are positive, then you may avoid negative energy.

- **Subjectively Negative**

Is it really something negative that you're observing, or is it only a negative instance to you? Take meat-eating, for example. You may be a vegan who firmly believes that non-vegetarians are what is wrong with the world. However, most of the world's population (more than 80%) consumes meat and animal products; thus, eating meat isn't a negative trait in the grand scheme of things.

To summarize the techniques of identifying negative energy, you should always know the signs to look for and to avoid. Negative energy is generated through negative afflictions, thoughts, emotions, or occurrences. You can point out the presence of negative energy through three different mediums, namely, yourself, the people around you, and your surroundings. Remember that emotions are the best and easiest way to identify negative energy in a place or person.

Chapter 3: Before You Start

Although a simple smudging ritual consists of easy steps and requires just a few supplies, the technique's effectiveness depends on some preliminary arrangements. In addition to finding and arranging a sacred space to carry out the smudging process, you also need to clear your mind, ground yourself and set the intentions in your special space. This can include creating an altar or simply setting up the smudging space with the necessary supplies.

Creating a sacred space is an essential part of the process that should not be skipped if you want the process to be effective. Setting the intentions for the ceremony is also a crucial step, as it helps create a spiritually charged atmosphere. Once this is done, the respective invocations are said, and the smudging process begins.

However, before learning about that process, you must know how to prepare your space and *when* to perform this technique. This chapter will include a guide to the preliminary groundwork required for smudging rituals, followed by instructions on when to practice these rituals.

Creating an Altar

An altar is a space designated to honor the spirits, universe, and other divine beings.
https://unsplash.com/photos/WzrOg4YzJ5w

Smudging is a deeply spiritual process, and, as with any other divine process, it requires a sacred space where it can be performed. This is where an altar comes in, which, in essence, is a space designated to honor the spirits, universe, and other divine beings. It's a place where you make offerings to the spirit world and express gratitude for your blessings. If you have any experience with other esoteric practices, you'll know the significance altars are usually given.

On the other hand, if you're just starting out on your spiritual journey, the thought of creating an altar may seem intimidating at first. However, it's a creative process that helps you express your inner soul. In fact, on a subconscious level, any time you place beautiful pieces on your mantel, table center, or shelf, you're essentially creating an altar. In this sense, you're already creating little altars around your home whenever you group together objects you love.

Your smudging altar can either be generic or specific to the intent of your ritual. For instance, if your intention is to attract better health or welcome love, your altar should be decorated keeping this in mind. You may think altars are just decorative spaces, but they're so much more. They need regular energetic movement and care, so when you do create an altar, it becomes your responsibility to care for it daily. The key to creating the most energy-filled altars is to be specific and conscious when you're setting it up. For instance, if you're creating an altar for spiritual protection, you must decorate it with crystals and other spiritual tools associated with protection and set the intentions accordingly. As a result, your sacred space will develop the power needed to complete your goals.

The best part about creating an altar is that no specific rules are involved. Your altar is a sacred space that is your own and should be an expression of your intentions and energy. This means the more empowered you are while creating your altar, the more power will be imbued in it. If you're an absolute beginner, you can follow a set of guidelines to make the process easier for you. Here are some steps you should consider:

1. **The Area**

    Choose the area and surface of the altar in a place where you will not get disturbed. This does not specifically have to be a designated altar space and can be as simple as your bedside table or the windowsill. You can even use extra space on your bookcase as your smudging altar or create one on the fireplace mantel. Of course, this doesn't mean you can't set up a separate space with a table prepared just for this purpose. Wherever you decide to set up this stage, you should keep in mind that smudging produces smoke that needs a place to escape. Your room should have windows and doors for ample ventilation. Remember to keep these open when you're performing the smudging ritual.

2. **The Theme**

    If you have a particular intention for which you need to perform the smudging process, it's best to design your altar according to that theme. For instance, you may need more clarity in life or desire more energy or vitality. You may want to express or attract love and create powerful relationships or practice gratitude for the blessings in your life. Whatever the case, you can create an altar designed specifically with that intention in mind. The most common altar themes are love, gratitude, and connection.

3. **Spiritual Tools**

When you're performing smudging, you'll find that the space will be surrounded by a lot of spiritual energy. You can use energy enhancers and other spiritual tools to contain and enhance this energy near the altar. For instance, you can use a piece of fabric or a tray as the foundation of energy. On it, you can put candles, crystals, flowers, specific images, sculptures, and any special items you find in nature, like seashells, stones, etc. You will also want to designate a space on your altar to keep your smudging tools.

There should be a beautiful, restful space where you can put your smudge stick or palo santo in between smudging sessions. Other smudging tools can also be displayed on this altar. These can include smudging fans, feathers, abalone shells, etc. When these tools are kept on your smudging altar, they'll be kept safe and organized and accumulate power from their surroundings. Crystals are usually the most popular choice for altar setup, as they help you tap into the energy of your smudge tools. More on crystals in a later chapter.

Setting the Intentions

Every type of smudging ritual follows almost the same order, which starts with setting the intentions of the process. After the intention, spiritual energy is invoked, and the actual smudging process follows. Setting the intentions for a smudging process is one of its most essential steps. Without an intention, all kinds of energies are being attracted toward your space, which you want to avoid at all costs. Setting intentions does not have to be a super complicated process, where you use numerous tools or only speak in confusing tones and flowery language! It can be as simple as lighting a candle and speaking out your intention for the process, like, *"My intent for this ritual is to get rid of all the negative energy in my bedroom."* If you know any prayers or mantras, you can also use those to set the intentions of the ritual.

Having a clear picture of your intention and expressing it at the beginning of the smudging ritual is the first step in the process and should not be neglected. It's an empowering act of trust, focus, and surrender. So, take a few moments before any ritual to clarify your intent. Let the universe know what energies you want to invite into your life.

Gathering Supplies

The process of smudging and purifying your energy is surprisingly simple. In fact, you only need a smudge stick, a candle, a charcoal tablet, and two medium-sized bowls (one of them should be used to catch the flaming ashes falling from your smudge stick, while the other one should hold the smudge stick once you've finished the ritual). Both of these should be fireproof – try using ceramic bowls instead of plastic ones. After completing the process, you can fill the second bowl with sand so the smudge stick will be extinguished automatically. If you don't have access to sand, you can use salt in its place. However, try to avoid using water to put the flames out because this can create a harsh type of energy. Your smudging supplies should be kept on the altar you have created.

You can also add a smudging fan or feather to your supplies if you want to add to the value of the process. This is particularly helpful if you use sage bunches instead of the whole stick. Various beautiful smudging fans are available in stores and online; making them yourself is even better.

You can practice smudging in your home with sage, palo santo, or other herbs in two ways. The traditional method uses a smudge stick, while the lesser-used technique burns loose leaves in a fireproof bowl. If you don't have much experience with smudging rituals, it's best to stick to a smudge stick or sage branch rather than burning loose leaves. This is a comparatively straightforward process and does not require particular skills. You'll only have to worry about the ashes falling from the smudge stick and the risk of starting a fire. However, this problem can be easily remedied by keeping a bowl under the stick while smudging your space. Still, if you're nervous about the process, you should start by using just a few branches instead of the whole stick for the process. This will help you become more confident while you develop your smudging abilities. To get the branches, just unbundle a smudge stick and use a few of its branches to smudge your space.

The second option takes a bit more work than the traditional one, so it's best that you start with the easier one first and gradually move up to it. For this option, you will need a fireproof container to burn the loose herbs right inside the bowl. Although some people prefer to use abalone shells for this purpose, it is not recommended as they are not entirely fireproof. Instead, you can use those shells to display the sage leaves on your altar and use a simple ceramic bowl to burn them. Or, you could use abalone shells to catch the ashes falling from the burning leaves during smudging. Place some sand at the base of your fireproof container, followed by a charcoal tablet, and then put the leaves in place. Like smudge sticks, the loose-leaf blends also contain various herbs, including lavender, white sage, cedar, rose petals, juniper, and other herbs. You can either get a pre-made bundle of herbs or make it yourself.

When to Smudge

While there are no restrictions about when and where you can perform a smudging ritual, certain times are more suitable than others, depending on the intention. If you've never smudged your space before, now is a good time to start because your house has probably accumulated a ton of negative energy over the years. Even if you think you live in the most harmonious house, with the most positive interactions among your family, human energy creates a significant amount of energetic residue, similar to how dust accumulates in your home daily.

Regular smudging is a good habit, just like drinking a cup of tea in the morning or performing your workout routine. When you make tea for yourself every morning, you go through the movements of the process and take a moment to connect with yourself. This becomes a cherished ritual that is incomparable to any other activity. The feelings of calm and peacefulness are more about the rhythm of the ritual than the tea itself, and it is exactly the same when you establish another ritual.

Once you've developed the intuitive ability to be aware of the energy around you, you'll know exactly when you need to perform the smudging process. The need for spiritual cleansing can be a result of various things. For instance, a family conflict or some items you recently brought home, etc.

Life Situations That Smudging Can Improve

When your family is struggling, your space likely gets contaminated with negative emotions and energies. This is the best time to do a smudging ritual. You'll automatically become aware of the negative energies plaguing your house when you learn of this type of recent event. Smudging at times like this helps clear the energy after an argument and eliminates the tension between family members. You can also practice smudging if you or one of your family members are going through a difficult time in their personal life, at work, or at school, or is facing anything emotionally challenging. This practice can help you deal with heavy emotions like anxiety, depression, sadness, fear, and mental fatigue.

The low, stagnant, negative energies accumulating in a space can make it hard to breathe and make things worse for you. This is why smudging is essential, not just some spiritual voodoo people practice. The cleansing carried out by this sacred ritual helps you clear the way for a deeper, clearer connection to your inner self and the people around you. Think of it like this. Living in a house filled with negative energy is like trying to gaze at a beautiful garden through dirty windows. You cannot see anything clearly, even though the pretty flowers are right outside. To see the full beauty of the garden, you'd have to clean the dirty windows. Similarly, when left unattended, negative energies can gather in the deepest parts of your life and ultimately distort your view. Everyone is deeply connected by the energy of their homes, this is the place where you spend most of your time, and therefore, your aura is interconnected with your home's energy. When you clear and clean the energy around you, you're doing the same for the energy within you. So, whether you practice a simple or complicated version of a smudging ritual, it will help keep the energy in your home protected and pure.

Challenging Situations and Events That Would Require Smudging Your Home Include:

- A big fight
- Verbal or physical abuse
- Having rude guests
- The death of a family member
- Financial trouble
- An accident

- Relationship problems
- Illnesses

Whenever you're going through a tough time in your life, smudging can help clear out negativity and provide you with the support to get through the situation easily. Think of it in this way. Not clearing your house of negative energies is like eating breakfast on unwashed dinner plates. Would you eat anything served on a dirty plate? Most homes are filled to the brim with unwanted, negative energy, like the grime on these dirty dishes, which makes it very hard for people to be happy and healthy in these heavily toxic homes.

Many people emphasize the importance of decluttering a home to create a harmonious space, but they rarely talk about the energetic clearing of negative residues and imprints left in one's home. In fact, if you feel like there's ever-growing clutter inside your house that's proving impossible to clear, try to do a smudging ritual, and you'll see a notable difference in the energy flow of your home, making it easier for you to declutter. Smudging can also help with brighter instances, like when you're starting a new relationship, starting a new project, or moving to a new home. In these cases, smudging creates an environment filled with positive energy, which attracts all good things into your life.

Best Times of the Day to Smudge

Regarding energy cycles, a day has the same four cycles as the whole year. It moves from the depth of night (winter) to the morning (spring) to noon (summer), and finally, to the evening (autumn). This cycle is why so many people prefer to perform their smudging rituals in the early morning. There's something so calming yet invigorating about an early-morning smudging practice that starts your day on a most positive note. The best time to practice smudging in the morning is between 5 AM to 7 AM, during which time you can open up the energy channels from the universe and bring positive energy into your life. This habit of smudging is similar to smudging during the spring equinox. Plus, the morning practice helps you center your energy and makes you feel calmer. It opens you up to the possibilities of the day and prepares you to receive all kinds of positive energies.

Another good time to practice smudging during the day is between 11 AM and 1 PM. However, this doesn't seem as great as early morning smudging energy; it is said to be the most potent energy of the day – just like summer solstice is the best time for spiritual rituals. You can also enhance the effectiveness of your smudging rituals by incorporating the energy of seasonal and moon cycles. Working in harmony with the world's natural rhythms adds an energetic boost to your smudging sessions. However, you should note that considering these cycles is not necessary for your daily or weekly smudging routines. Using seasonal and moon cycles is especially helpful for larger smudging rituals when you have a specific intention in mind.

To determine the best timing for your ritual, start by clearly defining your intention. Are you looking to release and let go of negative energy, or are you seeking to invite specific positive energy into your life? Every smudging ritual involves clearing away negativity and welcoming positive energy. However, having a well-defined intent for a specific smudging ritual will help direct the energy most beneficially. Aligning the timing of your smudging with your intent will give your ritual an extra boost.

This chapter has covered the essential preparations required before engaging in the smudging process. Before embarking on this ancient practice, it is crucial to ensure proper preparations are undertaken to create a harmonious and sacred environment. By embracing these preparations, you can honor the ancient smudging traditions and create a sacred space for spiritual growth and healing. Smudging is a powerful tool for clearing negative energies, restoring balance, and inviting positive vibrations into your lives.

Chapter 4: Herbs, Resins, and Oils

The variety of herbs, oils, and resins used for smudging seems unlimited, with herbs ranging from the commonly used ones, including sage, lavender, and juniper, to the less popular options like cedarwood, vervain, and rosemary. Your choice of products depends on different influences, but mainly on what's available in your area. You can choose to use just one herb or create a smudge stick with a combination of different herbs. This is where your intuition will guide you, and some guidelines will give you the basic framework for selecting the products to use in a smudging ritual. This chapter is all about selecting herbs, resins, and oils for different types of smudging routines. It will also include a step-by-step guide to using resins, essential oils, and other products to practice a smudging ritual.

Choice of Herbs

Although there are no specific rules when making herb combinations for smudging, you should know what were considered the four sacred medicines in Native American traditions – tobacco, cedar, white sage, and sweetgrass – are never mixed. Other than this one rule, there are no limitations. Below are the most popular herbs, along with their specific properties. Your choices primarily depend on these properties and how they align with your intentions.

1. Cedar

The cedar tree.
https://unsplash.com/photos/r3_ZiorB_Ik

The cedar tree is one of the oldest trees on this planet; as such, it is potent, full of spiritual energy, and majesty. This herb has been associated with protection and cleansing and used for smudging and other spiritual purification processes by many Native American tribes. Cedar is considered to be a powerful healing herb and a guardian spirit that protects your home.

2. Juniper

Juniper is an ancient herb with strong properties of protection and blessings.
https://unsplash.com/photos/zVsQmJEd_DA

Dating just as far back as the cedar tree, juniper is an ancient herb with strong properties of protection and blessings. Many tribes have used it for protection rituals and to attract abundance and blessings into the home. The smudging energy of juniper can also calm and purify your space and brings positive energy to an otherwise negatively charged space.

3. **Lavender**

Lavender has soothing properties and is used in many natural herbal remedies.
https://unsplash.com/photos/Tinbs_bjKxA

Lavender has been used in smudging rituals for a long time. As you may know, lavender has soothing properties and is used in many natural herbal remedies. However, did you know it's also a very popular smudging herb, providing a sense of calm and clarity? It helps relieve stress and provides your space with sweet, nourishing energy. Burning lavender is also preferred as an after-smudging ritual to form a final protective shield around your space.

4. Pine

Pine helps deepen your breathing and makes your head feel clearer and more focused.
https://unsplash.com/photos/78EiTnCtn5U

Pine has a deeper effect on people rather than the space itself. It can help deepen your breathing and make your head feel clearer and more focused. It grounds and centers you. This herb is used to help bring forgiveness during difficult situations.

5. Sage

Sage helps bring clarity, peacefulness, and protection.
https://unsplash.com/photos/96zlc1Bt51w

Sage is the most popular herb for smudging rituals. When you hear the word smudging, the first herb that comes to mind is sage or white sage. This herb brings clarity, peacefulness, and protection. You can also use it to invoke the blessings of the divine universe. In addition to white sage, some other varieties exist, including black sage, purple sage, and blue sage. In fact, there are almost 300 varieties of sage. However, they're not all commonly used for smudging purposes.

6. **Sweetgrass**

   Sweetgrass, another popular smudging herb used for centuries, provides all sorts of benefits. Its vanilla-like aroma evokes a sense of trust, clarity, and peace. It resembles a sweet, nourishing, gentle presence, often associated with motherly energy. Native people call it the hair of Mother Earth. Traditionally, sweetgrass smudge sticks are created by braiding three strands of this herb, each representing kindness, love, and honesty.

7. **Rose**

   Rose petals are usually used in combination with lavender to create beautifully scented smudge sticks. Rose petals add a touch of graceful energy and attract love, healing, and harmony. They can also be combined with rosemary, thyme, and wild sage.

8. **Rosemary**

   According to ancient smudging traditions, rosemary has the power to protect your space from negativity while also cleansing it. Since it is a very energizing herb, it's usually combined with sage and other herbs for the best results.

9. **Thyme**

   Thyme is frequently used in conjunction with rosemary to purify and safeguard. It also enhances vitality, courage, and confidence while soothing the energy of sadness.

Although most combinations work well, you should listen to your intuition when making smudging combinations. Although you're encouraged to make herb combinations, it is suggested that you do not use too many herbs in a single combination as that can mix up their properties.

Burning Sacred Resin

Burning resins is another ancient ritual, which is very similar to smudging, if not even more powerful. Sacred resins are obtained from healing trees – the most popular ones being copal, frankincense, and myrrh. Each of these has unique properties, and at the same time, they provide almost the same benefits. Frankincense has protecting, cleansing, and uplifting properties, myrrh is used to clear confusion and align a person to the sweetness of their heart, and copal is used to clear the mind, eliminate any energy blocks, and attract positive energy into your life.

All three of these resins have in common their ability to cleanse and protect, which opens up the way for positive energy. Whether you want to attract love, abundance, inner peace, or better health, these resins can be used to provide the same properties as burning herbs. These resins are usually combined to make up a more potent solution, and other herbs are sometimes added to the mix. As with all herbs, oils, and resins, setting your intention before the process is essential.

Although resin is a better option for smudging if you don't like the smell of burning herbs, it also requires some extra work. You must put in some time and effort to gather the necessary supplies. You should try this, especially if you've never done it before, because the fragrance of burning resin is wonderful! The aroma is said to connect you with the ancient roots of this universe and bring out deep emotional feelings. Many find the process to be incredibly grounding and, at the same time, deeply mystical. These are the supplies you'll need for burning sacred resins:

- A fireproof, heat-resistant bowl
- A bit of sand to place in the bowl
- Incense charcoal

A pair of tongs Your choice of sacred resin A candle Here are the six steps for burning sacred resin:

1. Gather your supplies and keep them in a place within reach. Make sure they're on an even surface to avoid a mess. Your altar would be a great place to start.//
2. Fill the fireproof container with sand as you would with a regular smudging ritual.
3. Light the candle and hold the charcoal on top of the flame using the tongs.
4. Keep it there until it lights up or becomes reddish. Once that happens, place the charcoal on top of the sand in the fireproof bowl.
5. Make sure the charcoal is heated evenly, and it should change color. If it doesn't, try to heat the edges before you place it inside the bowl.

6. Once the charcoal forms a layer of gray ash when placed on the sand, you'll know it's ready to burn resin.
7. Finally, place a small amount of resin on top of the hot charcoal and enjoy its fragrance.
8. You can keep adding small amounts of resin after it melts.

If you're just a beginner with resin smudging or even regular smudging, it's best not to move the bowl around too much on your first few attempts. Simply place it on an even surface where there's no risk of it falling. After you've become more accustomed to the ritual, you can try moving it around the room and to and from different rooms. However, place the fireproof container on top of a small tray to keep it stable.

Do not use abalone shells instead of fireproof bowls, no matter how aesthetically pleasing or ritual-like it looks. The shell is not fireproof and will get damaged. You could instead opt for censers. There's a wide range of censers available in the market, from the huge ones you see in churches and temples to the smaller ones used in homes worldwide.

You may struggle a bit with burning resin at the beginning. For instance, the charcoal may not light up easily or uniformly. However, with some trial and error, you will get the hang of the process, no matter how complicated it may sound at first.

Liquid Smudging

Liquid smudging is the easiest way to smudge without having to go through too many steps. Although the effects of this type of smudging are not the same as traditional smudging rituals, since it lacks the fire element, you will be creating a significant change in your home's energy when you practice liquid smudging. The process involves using a mixture of essential oils in pure water, the most popular combination being palo santo and white sage. You'll also find a variety of other mixes containing a range of essential oils on the market, or you can even make them yourself. In contrast with traditional smudging, you'll find various options for oils and liquid mixtures since this option is becoming increasingly popular, with most people opting for this low-effort smudging alternative.

The best thing about this technique is its portability; you can take it anywhere with you without worrying about fire safety. Plus, it's a quick process as compared to regular smudging, and it does not create smoke. So, you can even use it in your workplace, car, or hotel room. Even if you don't want to shift completely to liquid smudging, you can still opt for it sometimes while you're traveling or for a quick fix. You don't have to pick a single option and can choose multiple smudging techniques to incorporate into your routine, be it traditional, liquid, or other kinds of smudging rituals.

Natural Incense

The art of making incense is an ancient craft that has been carried out for spiritual purposes all over the world. These powerful solutions are created by following complex recipes and formulas for various spiritual rituals originating from ancient Egypt, Nepal, India, Tibet, and Japan. Since this practice has become very popular these days, many low-quality incense products are being sold. However, these products can easily be created by following a potent recipe of natural ingredients. Various incense products are available on the market, ranging from thin sticks that come in different lengths to small cones, rectangular bricks, incense coils, and even small, twisted ropes. There's even a wide variety of incense holders available in all shapes, sizes, colors, and materials.

If you've had any experience with burning incense, you're probably familiar with how frustrating those thin incense holders are. Once the incense sticks are done burning, there's ash scattered everywhere, creating a mess all around. Though you can opt for the wide incense holders, you can also try another, more spiritual technique of burning incense. You can create the base of the incense holder with some food material, like rice or grain, and place the incense sticks within this pile. This process not only helps spiritually cleanse your space, but the food also acts as an offering to the universe. Once the incense is done burning, you can mix its ashes with the grains or rice and place a new one in its place. In this way, you can also use several incense sticks simultaneously for a more purifying effect. If you want to select the best incense, buying it in person instead of ordering online is best. You'll have a direct experience with the fragrances of each product and find the product that is most suitable for you.

Essential Oils

The use of essential oils for smudging rituals is a favorite among many, especially since so many varieties and diffusers are present. Ultra-sonic diffusers are all the rage today. They use a cold mist to diffuse the essential oils into the air, so the scent is comparatively stronger than many other candle diffusers. But perhaps the best part is that this requires little or no effort from you. All you need to do is fill the diffuser with cold water and the essential oils of your choice and select the function and timings. This is the simplest way to energize your space and put positive energy into the environment through essential oils. Like liquid smudging, this process doesn't require you to burn anything and is thus missing the element of fire. So, while it can't be compared to traditional smudging rituals, it's still something that can be done on a daily basis.

The cleansing happens on a more subtle level, but it does have a considerable effect on the negative energy in your environment, not to mention the added benefit of your space smelling wonderful. Here are some of the most popular essential oils that are used for energy clearing. You can use a combination of these oils or simply stick to one at a time as you see fit. Remember that you might not react positively to the herbs used in each of these essential oils. Therefore, you should read any health disclaimers provided with these products.

- **Balsam Fir Oil**

    This pure essential oil has numerous uses, from relieving muscle tension to fighting infections and purifying the energy in any space. It has a refreshing, uplifting scent and helps balance the energy around you. By using this essential oil, you will feel your breathing get deeper and begin connecting with your inner wisdom.

- **Cedarwood Oil**

    A soothing, grounding, and warming herb oil, the woody scent of cedarwood oil is unmatched by any other and can be used to clear the energy of any negative vibrations. You can use it to imbue your space with protective and peaceful energy. Cedarwood itself is considered to be a symbol of abundance and wisdom.

- **Cypress Oil**

    In addition to having numerous medical benefits, Cyprus oil is also a popular choice for smudging rituals because of its clear and energizing fragrance. It is said to be a holistic solution for mind and body healing. Thus, it helps relieve one's anxiety, stress, and other mental issues. When you use this to smudge your space, your space will become filled with calm and vitality.

- **Eucalyptus Oil**

Another essential oil mainly popular for its medical benefits, including antibacterial, antiviral, anti-inflammatory, and antimicrobial properties, eucalyptus oil, is a frequently used ingredient for smudging rituals. It helps rejuvenate your energy, improve your memory, and help reduce the tension in your space, resulting in a clear, cleansed environment.

- **Frankincense Oil**

Frankincense originates from the resin of Boswellia carteri trees gathered from the wild. Its beautifying and purifying properties have been revered for centuries. Frankincense provides a comforting yet invigorating energy, elevating the atmosphere of any area and creating a profound sense of wellness. It is believed to enhance memory, alleviate inflammation, and support restful sleep if used consistently.

- **Juniper Berry Oil**

Juniper is renowned for its detoxifying and immune-boosting properties. In addition to its capacity to eliminate negativity and purify the surrounding air, juniper is highly soothing and helps you sleep better. The essence of juniper oil facilitates the dissipation of negative energy, providing a serene and safeguarded environment.

- **Lavender Essential Oil**

Undoubtedly, lavender stands out as not only the most popular but also one of the most versatile oils. Its remarkable cleansing, purifying, calming, and soothing properties harmonize with its revitalizing and energizing capabilities. Lavender, an adaptogenic herb, adapts to your energy level, delivering what is needed to restore balance, whether it requires activation or peace. For those new to essential oils, lavender is unquestionably the ideal choice to use in the beginning.

- **Palo Santo Oil**

Palo Santo embodies a unique duality of being uplifting yet grounding. Its exceptional power lies in its capacity to cleanse and purify by transforming low and negative energies within a space or an individual's energy field. Additionally, palo santo imparts a gentle and tranquil aura of peace. It is frequently employed in ceremonies to facilitate participants in achieving profound states of meditation and fostering a deep connection with the universe.

• **Peppermint Oil**

Peppermint oil has the remarkable ability to quickly alleviate tension within the body and the surrounding environment. Its cleansing and invigorating properties refresh the air, clear the mind, infuse the space with revitalizing energy, and evoke a sense of renewal and optimism. When creating essential oil mixtures, peppermint oil proves to be one of the finest additions, as it harmonizes seamlessly and enhances the effects of most air-purifying oils.

• **Pine Oil**

Pine oil has a fresh and empowering aroma accompanied by a calming and uplifting energy. Not only does it possess anti-inflammatory properties, but it also helps alleviate headaches and purifies the air by eliminating pathogens. Using pine oil can effectively transmute negative energy, creating a renewed sense of hope and rejuvenation.

• **Rosemary Oil**

Rosemary is a revitalizing essential oil that excels in purifying and energizing. It helps relieve stress, enhances mental clarity, and strengthens the immune system. As a member of the same family as lavender and sage, rosemary shares their remarkable ability to clear negative energy and instill a profound sense of peace.

• **White Sage Oil**

White sage is renowned for its revitalizing and purifying properties and its ability to cleanse negative energy. Its earthy aroma has a calming effect on the mind and can alleviate fears and anxiety. Additionally, white sage possesses antibacterial qualities that help fight infections. Throughout history, white sage has been widely used for its profound energetic and healing benefits.

Before you engage in smudging rituals with herbs, essential oils, and resins, consider a few disclaimers regarding fire safety and potential allergies. When working with open flames, exercise caution and ensure that you have a fire-safe container to catch any ashes or embers. Be mindful of your surroundings and keep flammable items away from harm. Additionally, remember that certain herbs and botanicals can trigger allergic reactions in some people. If you have known allergies or sensitivities, it's advisable to perform a patch test or consult a healthcare professional before using specific herbs or essential oils.

Chapter 5: How to Smudge

Smudging your home, items, and yourself with herbs will raise the vibrations of the object being cleansed.

https://unsplash.com/photos/x5hyhMBjR3M

Now that you've thoroughly familiarized yourself with the background and basic tenets of smudging, you can examine the foundational steps and structure of a smudging ritual. This chapter provides general guidelines to follow. However, everyone will use a different technique. You'll also receive tips and instructions for an all-encompassing smoke bath and techniques for smudging objects.

The Basic Steps of Smudging

Smudging your home, items, and yourself with herbs will raise the vibrations of the object being cleansed. Below are the basics steps for smudging.

1. Setting an Intention

Although it's recommended that you establish an intention during the preparatory phase, it's not too late to do it as the first step of the smudging ritual itself. This can be done silently or aloud and as simply or elaborately as you want. Feel free to be as creative with your intention as you wish. Reasons for smudging can vary from wanting to clear negative energy to inviting positivity and blessings to connect with the higher self or nature to a desire to enjoy the beneficial essence of herbs in the air. Once you've set your intent, aim to keep it in focus during the entire ritual.

If you have trouble focusing on your intention, try using a focal point to enhance your concentration. For example, some practitioners find gazing at the smoke beneficial for keeping their concentration focused – a fundamental element during spiritual work. Others will visualize their intention. To do this, take a few moments to close your eyes and see all the negative energies in your space, self, or object released through the open windows and doors. Or, imagine white or gold light entering the fresh air and filling every corner of your space with its peacefulness.

Creating a mantra is another way to channel your intention and invite positive vibrations into your home. Create a simple mantra you can repeat to yourself, like "*This space/object/person is full of calmness and light,*" or "*All negativity be gone from here.*"

2. Invoking Spirit Guides, the Four Directions, or Higher Self

Invoking spiritual help is fundamental for purging rituals, especially when smudging for psychic protection and energy clearing. Choose who you want to summon and for what purpose, offer a prayer or affirmation of gratitude, or ask for protection from negative energies. You can also light a candle and focus on inviting your spirit guides into your space, then blow out the flame to signal the completion of this cleansing stage. The same applies when you want to tap into your higher self. Determine why you want to seek information for your inner spiritual entity and ask it to reveal itself.

Here is an example of a prayer you can use to invoke spirit guides:

"As I light this sacred herb, I ask you to join me,

To cleanse this (space/object/person/myself) and protect it from intrusions.

I ask you to help me heal and find strength and peace.

As the sacred herbs burn."

According to Native practitioners, the four cardinal directions have a unique significance in smudging. Consequently, it's fundamental to invoke them properly before the ritual. Here is a rundown of what the four directions represent:

- **East:** Associated with the new light of the day, which arises when the sun rises above the horizon in the morning. The East is believed to help manifest new beginnings and growth opportunities and channel wisdom.
- **South:** As the sun peaks, it emits most of its warmth. The south might also represent the earth, the most productive phase of the year, or a stage in someone's life.
- **West:** Attributed to maturity, the West is where the sun sets. As it dips below the horizon, the sun signals the end of the day. Similarly, this direction can signal the end of a journey or process.
- **North:** Connected to guidance and wisdom, the North is one of the quintessential directions. Encompassing the other three elements, the North represents the trials and tribulations one experiences during their life journey.

You can use different methods to honor the four elements, including the following prayer:

"I call on the spirits of this herb to ward off negativity from around me, seen or unseen.

I call on the spirit of the East, who brings air, to grant me peace and inspire me during this ritual.

I call on the spirit of the South, who brings fire, to empower and protect me.

I call on the spirit of the West, who brings water to cleanse and purify the object of the ritual.

I call on the spirit of the North, who brings the earth, to help me ground and enhance my intention.

I ask you all to look over me from above as I do my work.

I ask nature to guard me from below until all negativity is gone.

Thank you, elements and nature!"

3. Clearing

Clearing refers to the actual act of smudging oneself, the space, or the object that needs to be purged of negativity by waving the smudge stick around the area or object. Using a feather or fan helps to direct the smoke as needed. Alternatively, you can use your hands to move the smoke around. However, before you get to this, you must light the herbs. When using a smudge stick, hold one end over the flame until it flares up. Gently blow out the flame. Your plants should glow with a scintillation of orange light and have a steady stream of smoke emanating from them. Start steering the smoke around the object you are cleansing your space, yourself, or any item you wish to purge from negative energies.

4. Moving Mindfully

While smudging, it's essential to move mindfully and with intention. Don't worry - there isn't a right or wrong way to smoke cleanse your property or person. It's all about being aware of the energies. When purging a space, start at the main entry point, and move toward the corners. If purifying your entire home, take your time with the places you use often as well as the corners of rooms. Low vibrational energy often hides away in inaccessible areas. When cleansing yourself or an object, move slowly, pay attention to every detail, and spend extra time on the areas that feel weighed down with negativity.

Moving mindfully and with raised awareness is also a chance to make this practice more personal. Only you know what helps you focus and lets your energy flow. Everyone will approach smudging a little differently because they have distinct personalities. Accordingly, everyone requires different forms of mindfulness. If you try working mindfully in a certain way and it doesn't work, find something else that does allow you to clear your mind and work efficiently.

5. Closing the Ritual with Blessings

To bring a space cleansing ritual to a close, smudge around the four corners of the space, then seal the doorways with a prayer, mantra, or another tool (like salt or crystals) to keep any negative energy out and protect your sacred space. Or, you can go around the object or person you're cleansing, moving clockwise – or imagine a shield forming in the same direction if you're cleansing yourself. Express gratitude for the elements, the spiritual guides, and nature before extinguishing your smudge stick.

Take as long as you need to say thanks for all you have and the blessings you'll receive in the future. Thank the refreshed energy now residing in you, your tools, your space, or another person. As you reflect on your ritual, appreciate that negative energy is no longer blocking the flow of positivity, and embrace the opportunities this offers. When you're ready, take a deep breath and let your mind fill with your normal thoughts as you slowly return to your day-to-day activities.

Bonus: Techniques and Tips for Taking Smoke Baths and Smudging Objects

Cleansing objects, spaces, and people can be a fantastic way to reclaim the energy within them. Smudging can protect you from any negative vibes accumulated in them due to their interactions with negative energies. You can combine smoke-cleansing with other energy-boosting or exchanging methods like prayers, affirmations, sounds, essential oils, smudging with herbs or incense, visualization, or chanting. Below you will find step-by-step instructions and tips for cleansing any object, space, or person.

Smudge Ritual for Large Objects or Spaces

Cleansing bulkier items or pieces of property requires more energy. This ritual's recipe includes multiple dried herbs – depending on your needs, you can choose whether you want to use all or just some of them.

Ingredients:
- Basil
- Pine cones
- Cloves
- Lavender
- Rosemary
- Juniper
- Sweetgrass

- Cedar
- Palo santo
- Garden sage
- White sage

Instructions:
1. After opening windows, cleanse the object or space physically. Make sure it is free of debris and dust before you move on to smoke cleansing.
2. Select an intention (preferably in the form of prayer or affirmation) that resonates with your goals and recite it aloud while focusing on the object you are cleansing. For example, you can say something like:

   "I purge this object of all energy that doesn't belong here."

   "I want to fill this space/object with positive, soothing energy."

   "I am cleansing this space/object of negative energy to let in love and light."
3. Bind the herbs in a bundle and light them from one end until they give off smoke. Call on a spiritual helper you wish to channel and acknowledge the four directions.
4. Smudge an object by moving it above the smoke in a clockwise direction. As you smudge around the item, focus on releasing any negative energies that may have been left behind and inviting peace and love.
5. When cleansing a space, gently circulate the smoke with your hand, then move clockwise around the room to purify the desired area while repeating the intention.
6. Visualize the object/space surrounded by white light – symbolizing the renewed energy field now filled with positivity and protecting it from any unwanted energies.
7. This is also optional, but you can chant your mantras or words of power that are meaningful to you while focusing on the object/space. This will help raise its vibration and invite positive energy into your home. Or, you can keep focusing on your intention – do whatever helps manifest it more efficiently.
8. Finally, thank the spiritual source you worked with to help to cleanse this object or space and set a clear purpose for its future

use.

Smudge Ritual for Smaller Items

If your practice involves regular interactions with negative influences, a banishing ritual for cleansing your tools is a must-have. Or, if you've just bought an antique item and aren't sure of its origins, smoke cleansing will prevent it from tainting your space with potentially disruptive energies. The following ritual should be performed whenever you feel an object has accumulated low vibrations.

Ingredients:
- White sage
- A candle
- Incense of your choice
- A ceramic dish for the incense
- Sweetgrass essential oil

Instructions:

1. After opening the windows, light a white candle, hold up the object, and say:

   "I banish all negativity from this object. It's not welcome here anymore."

2. Then, trace a circle around the candle with your fingers, moving clockwise. Likewise, burn the sage, moving clockwise around the object while thinking about the positive vibes you want to surround it and what you plan to do with the re-energized item.

3. As you do this, visualize a protective barrier forming around the object. Finally, blow out the candle and say:

   "Negativity, I release you from this object. You're free to go."

4. Put the sage on a dish, place it in the center of your workspace, and leave it to burn. It will clear your space and protect you from unwanted energies you freed from the object.

5. You can channel positive vibes toward the object now that you've released the negative energy. Sweetgrass can attract positive energy – so applying 10 to 20 drops of sweetgrass essential oil in a diffuser should do the trick. For optimal effects, do this every time you smudge.

A Smoke Bath for Improving Energy Flow

This smoke bath is designed to boost the energy flow through your entire chakra system. By taking it, your space and belonging will be cleansed of negative energies, and your physical, mental, and spiritual health will be restored.

Ingredients:
- Herbs or smudge stick of your choice (for example, sage, palo santo, or sweetgrass)
- An abalone shell (or, alternatively, a clay bowl)
- Matches
- A feather (optional if you do not want to use your hand)

Instructions:
1. To begin with, start by creating a soothing environment. Peace and tranquility will help you focus. This can be achieved with essential oils like lavender or chamomile, dimming the lights, playing soft music, burning incense, or any other measures that help create a calming atmosphere.
2. Think about the result you want to manifest. Be concise and honest when formulating the intention – as this is the most critical element of the ritual. It will also determine what other tools you need to support your purpose and work effectively.
3. Open your windows and keep your smudge stick or herb bundle smoking.
4. Next, take some deep breaths to relax your body and mind. You'll start by cleansing yourself – before moving on to objects and your environment. This requires intense focus.
5. Use a feather or your palm to waft the smoke around your body – from the top of your head to your feet.
6. Pay attention to your breathing – keep it slow and steady. If you wish, you can remain connected to your breathing by visualizing your intent.
7. As you breathe in, imagine all the negative energy entering your body, leaving you feeling relaxed and refreshed. As you breathe out, imagine releasing all this negativity away from you. Continue to do this until you're in a completely relaxed state.

8. Now it is time to open up and release all stagnant energy within yourself. To do this, recite the following affirmation:

"I am opening my mind, body, and soul and releasing all the stale energy within it."

9. Visualize a powerful light radiating from the center of your chest, slowly expanding and purging your energy field. Do this until you feel you're free of any negativity.
10. The next step is reinforcing your smudging effort with positive affirmations or prayers. You can also use sound vibrations to foster additional cleansing and balance the energy fields during smudging. Use tools that align with your vibrational frequency and force any stagnant energy to dissipate.
11. Then, start walking around slowly, and carry the smoke to each spot you want to cleanse. Once again, move the smoke around the area with your hand or a feather. Focus on places where energy could escape or hide, like windows, doorways, hallways, pieces of furniture, or plants. Use the principle from the step above for cleansing objects and tools.
12. As you watch the smoke, you might notice that it changes direction or behavior when it touches certain things. This could indicate that you should pay closer attention to these items or areas.
13. Try not to breathe in the smoke – or fill your entire space with billowing smoke. Remember, you're doing a smoke bath, not fumigating your property.
14. Seal the energetic entry points once ready to wrap up the cleansing ritual. You can do this by taking a deep breath and visualizing a powerful light radiating from the center of your chest, slowly shrinking until all your energy is fully contained within. As you do, say:

"The entryway is closed for negativity, and everything and everyone is protected."

15. Affirming the results of the smoke bath will help keep negative energies away from you so that you can remain in an open state for positive energies.

What to Do if Your Smudge Stick Goes Out

You should avoid letting the smudge stick or bundle go out during a ritual. Keep an eye on it and blow on it gently as soon as you notice it's not glowing anymore and the smoke is decreasing in intensity. It's not the end of the world if it goes out; keep your matches at hand to relight the herbs if necessary. Some herbs are harder to get burning and will die out more easily. This is normal - you'll have to pay more attention to them.

Another way to prevent smudge sticks from going out is to hold them at an angle while in use. If you have to relight the herbs, ensure the entire end of the stick remains engulfed in the flame for at least 20 seconds.

After concluding your ritual, put out the flames by pressing them in a waterproof container, abalone shell, or sink. Alternatively, you could blow on them, but some practitioners advise against this as they deem it disrespectful to the spirits. Likewise, it's not recommended to extinguish the embers with water either. Soaking the herbs could make it impossible to light them again.

If the herbs have burned down completely, or you want to banish a large amount of negativity they collected, bury them in the soil. Nature will help you dispel and neutralize those negative influences so they wouldn't come back to haunt you later.

Dealing with Stubborn Energies

In most cases, you will know that the cleansing process was successful by looking at the color of the smoke. For instance, if the smoke is thick and dark, there's a lot of energy left to clear, and when it becomes lighter, it means that the negativity is gone. However, this might not always be as easy. Some energies are so powerful and persistent that they will stubbornly cling to your objects, space, yourself, or those around you. In these instances, you should do a second (and, if needed, third) cleansing. When you do, pay attention to how the smoke moves. Does it cling to the object or parts of the space, trying to envelop it? Or is it trying to evade it? In the former case, there are still more negative energies lingering there, while in the latter case, the smoke moves away because all negative energies have been dispelled. If you're working in a room, open all the windows to let the smoke (along with the negativity) leave the space. If cleansing a non-stationary object, move it as close to the window as possible, so the tainted energy can leave immediately.

Incorporating Smudging into Your Daily Schedule

Most practitioners recommend smudging once or twice a month, depending on how frequently you encounter negative energies. However, if your practice involves regular spiritual work, you, your tools, your space, and those around you will be exposed to constant energetic interferences. To counteract their effects, incorporate regular smoke-cleaning rituals into your day-to-day life.

Wondering how to begin? It's easier than you think. Perform a quick smudging ritual every morning or evening – depending on when you work with spiritual energies. At the end of the week, do a deep cleansing of your tools, space, and, if necessary, yourself. Do additional purging tailored to specific situations. For example, if you've just hosted a large party and don't want the energies of all the attendees to taint your space, smudge them out. Smoke cleansing can also be a superb solution for clearing your aura after a disagreement with your employer or partner.

Chapter 6: Smudging Alternatives

Smokeless smudging methods can be useful when burning herbs is not practical or allowed in a particular environment. This chapter outlines various techniques and tools for energetic cleansing and purification without smoke – from sound healing through sprays and salts to visualization.

Sound Healing

Sound vibrations are a powerful tool for energy clearing and healing.
https://unsplash.com/photos/Hn4wYHOaeIc

Sound vibrations can be a powerful tool for energy clearing and healing. Vibration healing is a meditation or mindfulness technique which allows the participants to fully immerse themselves in higher vibrations, which carry beneficial energy. However, unlike similar methods, sound meditation can be done without setting an intention or needing outside guidance. Instead, you listen to sounds and let them soothe and heal your mind, body, and soul. This type of cleansing is particularly effective for extracting negative energy and promoting physical and emotional healing. Different sound tools like singing bowls, forks, gongs, chimes, and bells can be helpful when creating an environment for vibrational healing – also known as sound baths. Alternatively, sound baths can be concocted with calming music or pre-recorded sounds of instruments, nature, etc. The goal is to reach a deeper state of consciousness that promotes self-awareness, alleviates stress, and enables you to recharge with positive energy.

To use sound healing for cleansing, simply find a comfortable place to settle down. Close your eyes and begin to focus on your breath. As you breathe in and out, let the sound of the music or instruments permeate your senses – let it go beyond hearing. For example, you can visualize the sound waves entering your body and cleansing you from the inside out. Continue to breathe deeply and focus on the sound until you feel that you've been thoroughly cleansed.

You can also use this technique to energetically cleanse objects or spaces. For the former, place the item in a singing bowl (or near another sound source) and let the vibrations clear out the negative energy. For the latter, carry the sound source around the space. Stop a few times and let the sound rise three times in every corner or spot you stop at. Open the windows to let the negative vibes dissipate and avoid trapping them in the space.

Sprays

Smudge sprays are essential oil sprays or water-based mixtures infused with herbs or crystals conducive to purifying a space. There are different types of smudge sprays available, including:

- White sage, sweetgrass, and cedar mixture for purging negativity and replacing it with positivity.
- Essential oils of tobacco, cedar, sage, and sweetgrass for harnessing positive vibes from nature.

- Palo santo, sage, juniper, and lavender sage essences (often reinforced with rose quartz crystals) for another extra dose of positive vibes.
- Sequoia sweetgrass mixture for facilitating grounding and connecting with nature.
- White sage, hazel, cedar, and rosemary essential sprays (often enhanced with black tourmaline) for sacred rituals.

Using water alone to purify and cleanse objects, spaces, and people is a great way to sift out all the negative energies. Cleaning with water isn't just good for when you need to cleanse something or someone – but also when you want to dispel other people's tainted energies. For example, clean it before you start if you don't want anyone else's energy on a tool you prepare for a spell, ritual, or ceremony. However, for this purpose, smudge sprays work better than clear water. Similarly, you can cleanse a space or yourself with smudge sprays when you feel too much low-vibrational energy accumulated around you. If you regularly interact with different energies, do a smudge bath before going to bed or just after waking up to have a cleaner energy palette during the day.

Ingredients:
- Essential oils (use any oils mentioned above or any other one you prefer)
- Other herbal essences or herbs (you'll need to soak or cook them in hot water and let them cool down before use – in other words, make a decoction)
- Distilled water
- Pure alcohol
- Spray bottle (glass or plastic)

Instructions:
1. If you're using essential oils, pour 1.7 ounces of water into an empty glass, then add 20 drops of oils. Otherwise, use your decoctions.
2. Mix the alcohol with the water/decoction. The alcohol helps the liquid evaporate faster.
3. Pour the mixture/decoction into a diffuser or a spray bottle, then spray the room, space, or person you wish to cleanse while repeating your intention.

4. While you do, visualize white light radiating from the water, surrounding everything to restore the energetic balance.

When purging negative energies, finding the purest water source is crucial. This method uses distilled water. Nevertheless, if you have access to natural flowing springs or streams, feel free to use them. Their water comes directly from nature, so their effect will still be powerful.

Salt and Salt Baths

Salt is known for its cleansing properties and has been used to purge and clear away negative energies since ancient times. Many people still use salt to ward off negative energy. It acts as a barrier to any low vibrations that may be present. So, using salt to cleanse your space, personal items, spiritual tools – and even yourself – is a good idea. For example, sprinkling salt around your space or placing it in containers or pouches can help absorb negative energy. As an alternative, you can also use salt baths for energetic cleansing. Different types of salts have various benefits. For example, plain table salt and sea salt work best for simple cleansing rituals, black salt is a powerful energy blocker, and pink Himalayan and blue salt boost positive energy. Likewise, flaky salt is best for dispelling negative vibes and replacing them with positive ones. Do not use salt to purify silver items because it can cause rust.

Here is how to use salt for cleansing items or space:
1. Fill a small bowl with salt.
2. When cleansing your tools, place them on top or underneath the salt.
3. Leave them overnight and retrieve them the next morning. You'll have a cleansed object with refreshed energy.
4. When cleaning a room or house, mix salt with water and spray it around the space.

Here is how to cleanse your home with salt:
1. Pour a small amount of salt into a bowl and place it at your front door to stop negative energy from entering your home.
2. Remove all objects from the area you want to cleanse and dust the corners around the room, then sprinkle salt around.
3. Make sure the area remains undisturbed for a couple of days. Keep children and pets away from the salt.

The Benefits of Salt Baths

In baths, salt can be combined with any other natural cleansing agent. A salt bath can have different benefits depending on your ingredients and intention. Below are some of them.

A Balm for Your Nerves

Adding herbs to salt baths can soothe irritated nerves, restore the balance of hormones affecting the nervous system and diminish the effects of negative thoughts and emotions. All this has a wholesome influence on your overall health. Let's say you arrive home after a stressful day. You draw a salt bath, and as soon as you emerge in it, you can tune out all your worries and enjoy the soothing effects of the salt.

Lower the Effects of Stress Stimuli

Whether you feel ready to take in new sensory information or are already weighed down with what you are currently processing, sometimes, the sensory stimuli just keep coming, day after day. The environments you move in, the people you deal with, and the entertainment you consume are all packed with stimuli that affect your energy and mental state. Salt baths can help lower the energetic imprint of all those influences that threaten to disrupt your balance.

Flush Out Toxins

Soaking in the bathtub with salt water or other ingredients with antioxidant effects is far more effective than any other over-advertised detox method. It takes no time to draw water and toss in some salt and soothing herbs like rosemary, and you won't have to worry about any unwanted effects either. Spending only 20 minutes in a bathtub when you feel down will flush out all the toxins in your body, and your health will improve dramatically.

Purging Your Energy Body

Spiritual baths have a therapeutic effect on the balance of your entire energetic makeup. They replace stagnant or harmful energy with positive vibes and raise your vibrations. Salts, crystals, and essential oils are essential for cleansing your energetic body. Essential oils will also help you replace the flushed-out energy with renewed energy, especially if you spend at least 25-30 minutes soaking and relaxing in the tub.

Fostering Self-Awareness

Salt baths are a fantastic tool for creating the perfect atmosphere for contemplation. Since you're already relaxing and cleansing in your bathtub, you can also take time to do a little reflective investigation of yourself. You can ponder on your intention or think about your goals and desires. The latter works best for establishing a connection between your intuition and your higher self. You can use any exercise to gain more self-awareness and reveal your innermost desires.

Salt Water Bath to Ward off Negativity

With the following salt bath, you can relieve stress, pain, and fatigue, improve circulation, and cleanse the chakra system. It's also great for exfoliating the body, reducing skin irritation, and even healing minor injuries. While sea salt is the most effective for this purpose, you can substitute it with coarse sea salt if you don't have any available. It's a simple and effective method to ensure you'll never be affected by negative interference.

Ingredients:

- Rock or coarse sea salt
- Lavender or tea tree essential oil
- A bucket
- Lukewarm water

Instructions:

1. Make sure your bathtub is clean before you take a bath. Otherwise, residual negative energy can interfere with the bath ritual. Whether you want cleansing, protection, or healing, the number one rule is to start with a clean slate. Cleaning the bathtub and the surrounding area helps eliminate unwanted vibes from your bathroom, enabling the cleansing ritual to take full effect.

2. Pour water into a bucket until it is half full. Add the salt and a few drops of essential oils to the water. Stir until the salt has completely dissolved. While you do, establish a clear intention. Whether you want your energetic pathways cleansed, resolve negative situations in life, cleanse your body, mind, and spirit, or attract positive influences into your life – make sure you define it clearly in your mind before you even start preparing for your bath.

3. Alternatively, you can introduce music or guided meditation. Listening to meditation music or any other soothing music or even a guided meditation will help you relax and boost the

benefits of spiritual cleansing and protective baths. Alternatively, you can sing before and after the bath - there is a reason why some people love singing in the shower. It helps clear the space from negative energies that have exited your body, mind, and spirit and put them in a better mood.
4. You shouldn't focus on your phone or other electronic devices while taking a salt bath. Place the device playing the audio out of your reach.
5. Stand in your bathtub and slowly pour the salty water over your body, from head to toe. Avoid getting water into your eyes. Feel how it's cleaning you of negativity.
6. Once you've finished with the salt bath, rinse yourself off and wash your hair and body with natural soap and shampoo. The salt can dry out your skin and hair, so both will need replenishing with a good moisturizer.
7. Take your time reflecting on how you feel before and after taking the baths. Not all cleansing baths work for everyone. To establish if a particular one works for you, acknowledge what you need help with beforehand and observe the effect. Compare your results to how you felt before taking it.
8. You can repeat the bath two to three times a week, depending on how affected you are by negative energies.

When using essential oils and herbs, make sure you're familiar with their effects. Not all of them are safe for everyone, particularly if you have sensitive skin. Use only those recommended for baths. If you notice any adverse reaction from any of them, stop using them in your baths.

Visualization

Using the mind's eye to visualize a white or golden light clearing the space is another effective way to cleanse without smoke or sound. Visualization involves picturing yourself surrounded by white light or any other type of light you feel drawn to. As you envision the light surrounding you, you must focus on it cleansing your aura and washing away any negativity. Or you can also visualize the light entering your body and filling you with positivity. Alternatively, imagine the light purging objects, spaces, or another person. It all depends on your purpose. The goal is to tap into the creative parts of your brain and put aside the analytical thoughts. Using a visualization method to cleanse something or someone is a great way to get your creative juices flowing. If you're not used to visualization, it's better to practice it first for a few days before you try this cleansing ritual on any object or space.

You can do this by sitting outside in a calm atmosphere, closing your eyes, and imagining a white light descending from the sky and settling around you. Once you start feeling an energy shift, your process will be successful. The more you perform this exercise, the more effortlessly the visualized light will come to you. You can also bring other colors as well to your mind's eye.

Here's what the different colors signify:

- **White** denotes purity, peace, protection, and serenity.
- **Yellow** is associated with intellect, strength, and energy.
- **Orange** is linked to luck, confidence, and success.
- **Red** symbolizes passion, desire, power, strength, and vitality.
- **Pink** signifies peace, emotional support, compassion, and affection.
- **Purple** is attributed to wisdom, spiritual connection, and safeguarding.
- **Blue** denotes safety, protection, tranquility, and healing.
- **Green** brings luck, fortune, prosperity, abundance, balance, and healing.
- **Black** is connected to energetic shielding, binding, and warding off negativity.

You can use a color that resonates with you or when you require the properties associated with it. You can also try to visualize a combination of these colors to design and create the perfect visual. For example, you can imagine the color purple when cleansing an object and want to remove the stagnant energy. The same color will also improve your chances of connecting with the spiritual world while performing a divination technique. On the other hand, green will enable you to channel nature's energy during healing rituals. Visualize the shades that resonate best with your intuition and personal preference. Fortunately, there are no set-in-stone rules for visualizing. If your intentions are pure and you practice diligently, your efforts will pay off.

That said, here is a quick step-by-step guide for a cleansing visualization:
1. Sit in a quiet, comfortable place with no distractions. Take a deep breath, hold it briefly, and exhale. Repeat this two more times.
2. Now, close your eyes and picture a white light surrounding your body, rising all the way up to the sky. Deep down, you can sense that this light will cleanse your energy field and remove any negative or unwanted energies.
3. Visualize this light growing more intense and boisterous as it forms a grand orb around you. It moves up your body, starting at your feet and moving to your head. Then, it enters your body from your crown chakra and passes through each of the seven chakras, one by one.
4. Imagine this light flowing from your hands to the object you're holding or the space around you. See the light engulfing the item or space and absorbing all its negative energy.
5. Then, visualize this light immersing into the ground, taking the negative energy with it. Take a few deep breaths and allow yourself to relax with the knowledge that negativity won't disrupt your energy or the energy of the object or space you're cleansing anymore.
6. Once you feel thoroughly cleansed, you can open your eyes and resume your spiritual work or day-to-day activities.
7. Initially, it might take longer to channel all the negativity into the light. However, once you get the hang of this process, it'll only take a few minutes to cleanse anything you want with white or any other colored light.

Paper Cleansing

Paper cleansing is a unique smudging alternative geared toward personal purification rather than space or object cleansing.

Ingredients:
- A piece of paper
- A pen
- An incense stick (optional)

- A white candle
- Matches
- A fireproof bowl or plate (alternatively, you can use a bowl of water or a sink)

Instructions:
1. Light the candle and settle into a relaxing position.
2. Take a few deep breaths and start writing whatever comes to mind. Don't try to focus on anything – just record whatever thought or feeling comes naturally.
3. When using incense, light it and inhale its scent. Allow it to wash over your mind, body, and spirit.
4. Next, set an intention, and focus on it.
5. Bring the paper to the candle flame and burn it over the fireproof surface to avoid creating a fire hazard.
6. Visualize negativity leaving your mind, body, and spirit and getting lost in the air.
7. End your ritual with a prayer, a quick meditation, or a breathing exercise.

Chapter 7: Crafting Your Supplies

While all sorts of smudging supplies are available on the market, with so much overwhelming choice, there's nothing better than crafting your own supplies. To some people, this may seem like a waste of time and effort, but those who have truly practiced smudging, and other spiritual rituals, know the difference personalized supplies can make. You'll find all sorts of smudge sticks with different herbs and essential oils when you go to the market. Liquid smudging solutions are also abundantly present, and essential oils can be found at any local store. However, when you make your own supplies, you have the freedom to use the herbs and ingredients that are most suitable for you without having to settle for pre-made combinations. You can experiment with all sorts of herbs and choose the ones that fit your intention. You can also avoid the herbs and oils you're allergic to and those you simply don't like. There are too many pros and not enough cons to stop you from DIYing your supplies. Plus, making them is not at all difficult and can easily be mastered. This chapter will provide you with instructions to create different smudging supplies ranging from smudge sticks to smudging fans and essential oil blends.

Crafting Your Smudge Stick

The primary element you need for a smudging ritual is, of course, a smudge stick. Crafting a smudge stick is a pretty easy task, especially if you have experience with DIY crafts. Before you gather the supplies, you'll need to determine the length, thickness, and types of herbs you'll use for the smudge stick. You'll also need to get some strings to tie the bundle. The thickness and length of the smudge sticks depend entirely on you. You can make big smudge sticks with a thickness of about two inches and a length of 12 inches.

If you prefer smaller, daintier smudge sticks, the thickness can be reduced to 1 inch, and the length can be as short as three inches. People usually prefer bigger sticks when smudging a large area, as these bundles smolder slowly. On the other hand, if you just have to smudge a small room or a person, then a smaller bundle would work fine. If you're making smudge sticks for the first time, it's better to have a variety, so make both thick and thin smudge sticks just in case. The thinner ones will be best used when you're traveling or if you want to gift them to someone. The bigger ones work best for space clearing for larger spaces like a whole house or land.

Choosing something as simple as the string that will tie your smudging stick together holds significance. When the smudge stick is lit, the string will burn along with the rest of the bundle and should therefore be made from natural materials like hemp or cotton. You shouldn't use plastic strings as they release toxic chemicals when burning. The color of your string is completely your decision. Some people dye it in different colors, while others use simple undyed strings. The length needs to be much longer than your smudge sticks since it will be wrapped around the bundle several times and then tied to secure it. While the rest of the factors, like the thickness, color, and length of your smudge stick, is entirely up to you, the non-negotiable part is that your smudge stick should be secured correctly. The herbs often dry out and shrink, resulting in the sticks falling apart. To avoid this, you must tightly wrap the smudge stick with the string. Here are the supplies you'll need to craft your smudge stick:

- The herbs of your choice – you can choose from the list provided in the previous chapters but are not limited to just those herbs.
- A natural string, either colored or plain – avoid using synthetic strings.
- A pair of scissors – should be sharp.

Once you have your supplies, follow these simple steps.
1. Gather your supplies and find a flat surface to place them on. Start by separating the herbs and then arranging them in order of

length and thickness. If you're using a combination of herbs, you should arrange them in a way that looks visually appealing. Make sure you don't use too many varieties in a single smudge stick, as the spiritual properties of each herb might not complement the other herbs. Instead, stick to a maximum of five herbs per smudge stick to keep a balance. If you're using rose petals, place them at the very top of your bundle to create an attractive smudge stick. Keep the shorter herbs on the outside, while the longer ones should be arranged so they are on the inside of the stick.

2. Prepare the strings by cutting them to the correct length for each smudge stick, which should be at least five times longer than the length of your herb bundle. The strings will be used to weave a pattern within your smudge sticks; therefore, they should be long enough. Keep enough strings to tie all of your smudge sticks.

3. Hold the herb bundle together with your hands, and tie a knot at the stems to secure them. Wrap the string around this knot a few times before bringing the string from the base of the stems to the tip of the bundle while holding the bundle together with one hand. Then, reverse the angle and return the string to the bundle base. Do this several times until you get a crisscross pattern, as seen on many smudge sticks.

4. When you've finished making the pattern, tie another knot to secure the wrapping. To make the smudge stick more secure, you can make some loops with the string at the base of the stems and the same loops at the top of the bundle. You can create many other patterns using your creativity or by looking them up online.

5. Once they're done, place your smudge sticks somewhere in the shade to dry out. There are two ways you can dry your smudge sticks. You can place them on a drying rack or screen with good air circulation space or hang them from a cooking rack or any other hanging place. Just be sure to keep them away from the sun so that there's little to no light where you dry them. However, air circulation is essential. They will be ready to use in about 10 days.

How to Make a Smudging Fan

Next on your list of smudging supplies is the smudging fan, and contrary to what you may think, making smudging fans isn't a difficult process either. You only need creativity, feathers, and decorative elements to create an elaborative smudging fan. When it comes to making them, the sky is your creative limit. Some common items used to make smudging fans include beads, crystals, shells, twigs, cords, and leather pouches. In fact, you can use any piece of nature that speaks to you and can be attached to the fan, whether it's some twigs, pinecones, or even leaves. People have made ocean-themed fans with beautiful shells and dried sea vegetation adorning the surface. Forest themes are also common, with antlers, twigs, and small pinecones used to decorate the fans.

You can also decorate your fan with bright-colored feathers, tassels, and crystals. You can even use just one feather adorned with a crystal as your smudging fan. Using a smudging fan during the ritual significantly impacts the process, as compared to using just your hand to wave the smoke around. It brings light energy to the smoke and ensures that the smudging energy gets to every part of the room. You can use real bird feathers collected from the wild or artificial feathers to make your fan. According to ancient traditions, smudging fans used to be made from the whole wing of an eagle, so the concept of a smudging fan is to replicate a bird's wing. Here are the supplies you'll need for your fan:

- Variety of feathers (collected from walks in nature or purchased from a craft store)
- Small and sturdy branch, driftwood, or a piece of wood (2 to 5 inches long)
- Glue gun
- Cord made from leather or another preferred material

Decorative items like crystals, small beads, personal talismans, or other appealing items When you have all your supplies ready, follow these simple steps:

1. Gather the materials on a large, flat surface, ideally a kitchen counter or a craft table. You'll be using a glue gun to attach the decorations, so be mindful of protecting the surface from the hot glue.

2. Divide the materials into four portions, place the feathers on one side, the decoration items on another, and the branch to be used as the base and glue gun in the center.
3. First, you need to arrange the feathers for the fan. Start by separating the feathers based on size and color. It's suggested that you use the same color feathers for the fan, but you can also be creative.
4. Place the larger feathers at the back and the smaller ones up front. The arrangement should resemble a bird's wing. Ensure all the feathers are facing the same direction.
5. After you've arranged the feathers, pick up the branch, and work out which side of the stick will be used as the front side of the fan. Then, apply glue to the base and attach the feathers, one at a time.
6. Keep attaching the feathers side by side and then on top of one another until the fan has enough wings.
7. Now, take the leather cord, and wrap it around the branch, either completely or partially. This is up to you. Use glue to firmly attach the leather to the wood.
8. Finally, select the decorations you want to use, and visualize the design you want to create. Before gluing the items onto the fan, first place them in their planned positions, and see if the fan looks good. Then, you can glue each item onto the feathers.

Your smudging fan is ready! Place this on your altar, along with the rest of the smudging supplies. If you're traveling and need to carry your smudging fan with you, pack it properly beforehand, either with bubble wrap or plastic sheets.

Liquid Smudging

Liquid smudging is one of the easiest ways to rid your space of negative energy and replenish the positive essence in your surroundings. Many of you may have decided to opt for liquid smudging – as it doesn't require much effort or require you to deal with smoke. The best part? You can make your own liquid smudging blend by choosing between a selection of essential oils. Or, you can follow the recipe below to make a liquid smudge blend of lavender, white sage, and several other powerful herbs.

Here are the supplies you will need:
- 15 drops of cedar essential oil
- 4-ounce bottle
- 15 drops of lavender essential oil
- 4 ounces of pure water

25 drops of white sage essential oil Once you've gathered your materials, the rest of the steps are pretty simple:
1. Wash and dry your bottle to ensure there are no impurities in the blend.
2. Add the essential oils to the water and mix thoroughly.
3. Pour this solution into the 4-ounce bottle, and screw it closed.

Your liquid smudging blend is ready for use! Always shake the bottle before every application. To experiment with the recipe, you can change the base oil, which is white sage essential oil. It's best to avoid adding too many different essential oils into the solution if you do not want to get rid of the main tone of the blend. Some other essential oils that go well with white sage include:
- Frankincense
- Lemon oil
- Wild orange
- Lime
- Geranium
- Cedarwood
- Sandalwood

If you want to make a more powerful blend, you can add a bit of unprocessed sea salt to the mixture, as it is said to amplify the effect of space cleansing. Alternatively, you can add a small crystal to the liquid smudging bottle. To do this, you must first charge the crystal by letting it sit in a bowl of water under direct sunlight for three days. Then, you can use this solar-charged crystal – and even the water in your smudging blend. This will add the fiery energy of the sun to your blend and make it even more effective in dispelling the negative energies in your spaces.

Of course, you must ensure the crystal is small enough to fit inside the tiny bottle. If it doesn't, you can still use the crystal-charged water for the blend. This is because water has memory and can carry vibrations inside its medium. So, when you let it charge by using the crystal's energy for several days, it will contain the positive energies carried by the crystal. Another alternative is to use Agua de Floride, which is basically a blend of different floral essences and scents in an alcohol base.

This blend is quite popular for creating different essential oil blends or other holistic solutions. Many shamans use it to cleanse and purify their energy and to protect and ground their auras. In fact, you can use it without any other additions to clear your space of negative essences by spraying it into the air. This is especially helpful when you're on the move, in a new space, or simply cannot prepare for a full-fledged smudging ritual.

Essential Oil Blends

In addition to liquid smudging, you can create some essential oil blends for your aromatherapy diffuser. The only difference between the two is the addition of water, followed by the spraying process. When using a diffuser, there isn't much to worry about; just put these essential oil blends into the diffuser and let it do its job!

You'll need only two supplies to create your essential oil blends; a small bottle (preferably made with dark-colored glass) and your selection of essential oils. Mix the essential oils and pour them into the glass bottle to make the blend. You'll need to store these blends away from heat and sunlight, as that can weaken their potency. Below are some easy recipes of essential oil blends, perfect for promoting healing energy and protecting your space from negative energy:

Heavy clearing essential oil blend:

This blend can be used to clear extremely toxic and negative energies from your space and your aura. If this feels a bit too intense, you can try the other recipes first. You can also choose not to use all of the essential oils mentioned in the recipe and stick with just two or three of the options shown. Pour the essential oil blends into the diffuser bowl and enjoy the fragrance:

- 15 drops – lemon essential oil
- 5 drops – pine or juniper essential oil
- 10 drops – peppermint essential oil
- 5 drops – eucalyptus essential oil
- 20 drops – lavender essential oil

- 20 drops – rosemary essential oil
- 5 drops – rose geranium essential oil (optional)

Cleansing and attracting good energy blend:

This harmonious fusion of essential oils can work wonders in purifying your surroundings while effortlessly attracting positive energy. This blend can create an inviting and revitalizing atmosphere where freshness and positivity thrive.

- 25 drops – lemon essential oil
- 15 drops – grapefruit essential oil
- 10 drops – peppermint essential oil (optional)
- 30 drops – tangerine essential oil
- 15 drops – lavender essential oil

If the process of counting drops for your blend makes you anxious, rest assured that it's common to err on the side of adding more rather than less. There's no need to worry because you can hardly go wrong with it. So, take a deep breath, relax, and let the diffuser do its magic. If you feel the scent isn't strong enough, simply pause the diffuser and add a couple more drops of essential oil. It's as simple as that!

When crafting your own supplies for smudging, there's something truly special about doing it yourself. Not only does it let you add a personal touch and infuse your intentions with your personality, but it also brings a whole different energy compared to store-bought goods. Remember to give them the respect they deserve when storing your smudging supplies. Find a cozy spot on your altar or another sacred space to keep them. Treating them with care keeps their energy intact and ensures they're ready to bring you magic when needed. When you take the time to craft your own supplies for smudging and store them respectfully, you're creating a special bond with the tools of your spiritual practice.

Chapter 8: Psychic Protection Methods

Your energy is constantly under attack because people around you can send you negative vibes, consciously or subconsciously.
https://unsplash.com/photos/pIY5yM0bmMQ

You may not be aware of it, but your energy is constantly under attack. People around you can send you negative vibes, consciously or subconsciously. Some may do this to harm you or your loved ones mentally, physically, or spiritually. Even those closest to you can be secretly harboring feelings of anger, jealousy, or resentment toward you.

This negative energy can disturb your peace of mind and prevent blessings from coming your way. You shouldn't leave yourself vulnerable to psychic attacks. You can use various techniques with smudging to shield you from negativity and all the people who want to cause you harm.

This chapter will explain how to identify psychic attacks and provide techniques to defend yourself in these situations.

Signs You Are Under Psychic Attacks

Some physical and mental afflictions aren't medical. If you get checked up, do all the necessary tests, and find nothing is wrong, you may be under psychic attacks. Identifying the symptoms of these attacks will give you an idea of what you are dealing with so you can take precautions to protect yourself.

Bad Luck

If you are a victim of psychic attacks, you will feel like you are cursed or experiencing a series of bad luck. Negative energy and entities affect your aura and block your chakras, attracting negative experiences and preventing good fortune from entering your life. No matter what you do, nothing goes your way. It can sometimes feel like you are the unluckiest person on the planet. Your life will be chaotic. You will constantly fight with your loved ones, start acting differently, and won't be able to recognize yourself.

Nightmares

When you are asleep, you are in your most vulnerable state, and your auric field can be susceptible to negative energy. Nightmares, sleep paralysis, or night terrors are often signs of psychic attacks. Bad dreams can be so vivid that they terrify you. The situation can be so severe that you will dread going to sleep, making you feel exhausted the next day.

Exhaustion

Negative energy drains you mentally, physically, and emotionally making you constantly exhausted. You will lose your spark and will have no desire to chase your goals. You won't even have the energy to get out of bed. In severe cases, this can lead to isolation and depression.

Negative Thoughts

Naturally, negative energy will lead to negative thoughts. These thoughts can be so intrusive, resulting in unexplainable phobias and fears. Negative energy will manipulate your thoughts and emotions and create false narratives to distort your reality.

Constant Fear

Negative energy is like a hunter that wants to catch you at your most vulnerable moment. Therefore, it will play on your fears and even exaggerate them in your mind to make you easy prey.

Being Watched

If you constantly feel that someone is watching you to the point that it makes you feel paranoid, you are under psychic attacks.

Gifts

Strangely, you can experience odd emotional, mental, or physical symptoms after receiving a gift from someone.

Accidents

Psychic attacks can make you accident-prone. People experience small accidents occasionally, like falling in the bathroom, dropping and breaking a glass of water, or pouring coffee over themselves. However, if you experience these accidents more than usual and you begin to feel something isn't right, you could be influenced by psychic attacks.

Losing Stuff

Who doesn't lose their stuff? You have probably lost more white socks than you can count. However, if you have been misplacing most of your items, like your cellphone or laptop, lately, negative energy may have affected you.

Indecisiveness

Have you been struggling with making decisions lately? Psychic attacks can make it hard for you to tap into your intuition to take action or make the necessary decisions.

Pain and Illness

If you don't suffer from any medical problems yet get sick or experience sharp pain, you could suffer from psychic attacks.

Heaviness

Negative emotions are a hard burden to carry. Psychic attacks can make you feel like you are carrying the weight of the world on your shoulders.

There is no denying that symptoms of psychic attacks can be both frustrating and scary. Luckily, there are effective techniques that you can practice with smudging to shield yourself from these attacks once and for all.

Grounding

Grounding, also called earthing, is a process where you connect your body with the Earth to feel rooted to Mother Nature and bring balance and stability to your body and life. It is also a meditation technique that can make you mindful, aware of your surroundings, and focused on the here and now so you won't be preoccupied with negative thoughts. Grounding is an effective remedy against many symptoms of psychic attacks like anxiety, stress, fear, forgetfulness, and feeling overwhelmed. These techniques also connect you with your body and your five senses so you focus within and quieten the negative thoughts.

Grounding exercises give you control over your energy to unblock your chakras and allow positive energy to flow through you and heal your body, mind, and spirit. Grounding will reverse the effect of psychic attacks making you more secure, confident, balanced, and energetic, and improve your sleep.

Since you interact with different people daily, you can never know where the next attack is coming from. You need to protect yourself from this potentially negative experience. Several grounding techniques can act as shields so you can live your day-to-day life without worrying about the negative energy of others.

Grounding Technique

Instructions:
1. Find a quiet place outdoors, like in your garden or backyard, or you can go to the park or anywhere in a natural environment.
2. Stand barefoot with both feet firmly touching the ground.
3. Breathe in and out slowly and deeply for a couple of minutes.
4. Close your eyes and visualize roots coming from your feet and reaching the ground. They extend so far right into the earth's core.
5. Now, release the negative energy from your mind and body through the roots and into the earth.

Grounding Protection Technique
Instructions:
1. Sit or stand in a quiet place away from distractions.
2. Take a few deep and slow breaths.
3. Close your eyes and imagine a big protective ball of white light surrounding you, covering your whole body as if embracing you to keep you safe from harm.
4. Fill the ball with positive energy, light, joy, love, and other warm emotions.
5. Next, imagine dark entities, negative emotions, and thoughts as arrows attacking you from all directions.
6. If this image makes you tense, keep your breathing steady and calm yourself.
7. Now, imagine the arrows bouncing off the white ball. You feel safe and protected. Nothing in this world can ever harm you.

The 5, 4, 3, 2, and 1 Technique

This is a simple technique where you list different objects in your environment that you can experience with your five senses, starting from five to one.

Instructions:
1. Sit in a comfortable position and look around you.
2. In your head, list in your head five objects you can see.
3. Four objects you can hear.
4. Three objects you can feel or touch.
5. Two objects you can smell.
6. One thing you can taste.

Breathing Technique
Instructions:
1. Breathe in deeply while counting to four.
2. Hold your breath for seven seconds.
3. Breathe out slowly while counting to eight.

Feel your body moving with every breath, and pay attention to how it feels. Be present in the moment and notice how your body changes when you inhale, hold your breath, and exhale.

Shielding

Shielding is a technique that protects you from intrusive and negative energy. You place an invisible energy shield around you to keep you safe and prevent psychic attacks from getting to you. You must practice shielding techniques whenever you feel tired, drained, and emotionally imbalanced.

The idea of shielding can seem otherworldly, and you may think you need to be a psychic or have special abilities to protect yourself. However, this process is simple, and anyone can practice it. You are made of energy, so think of this shield as an extension of yourself. It is a part of you that always surrounds you while keeping you safe.

Similar to setting boundaries with people, a shield screens all types of energy you deal with daily and filters the bad energy out, only letting positive and warm energy in. So, no one can invade your energetic field without your permission.

There are various shielding techniques that you can easily practice, and they are all equally effective.

Shielding Visualization

Instructions:
1. Find a quiet spot and sit in a comfortable position.
2. Take slow and deep breaths, and imagine you are releasing the tension and stress in your body with every breath.
3. Keep breathing until you feel relaxed.
4. Close your eyes and think about creating a shield around you to protect your energy.
5. The shield will be made of warm and blue light since the color symbolizes protection.
6. Now, set an intention. You can say something like, *"I intend to create a shield made of wisdom, light, and divine love to keep me safe from negative entities and intrusive energy."*
7. Next, visualize multiple mirrors facing outward, surrounding you from all sides, above and under you. Any negative energy that tries to come near you will be reflected back by the mirrors.

8. You have now created an energy shield that is sealed from all directions keeping you safe at all times and preventing any negativity from coming near you.
9. Now, set another intention that you will only allow positive energy and emotions to enter through the shield. You can say something like, *"I set an intention for only joy, love, and positive emotions and thoughts to pass through my shield."*
10. Visualize a rose quartz crystal radiating warm and pink light. The light is all around you, embracing you and making you feel loved and protected.
11. Now, your energy shield is complete. Sit for a couple of minutes while thinking of your intention. Enjoy the feeling of protection.
12. Memorize how the shield feels and think of this feeling whenever you are around negative people.

Jaguar Meditation

In different cultures, the jaguar is a symbol of protection.

Instructions:
1. Sit in a comfortable position in a quiet space.
2. For this technique to work, you should be calm and relaxed. You can place a few drops of essential oil in a diffuser and place it where you will practice this technique to keep you calm and reduce stress. You can also practice the 5, 4, 3, 2, and 1 breathing exercise.
3. Once you feel calm, close your eyes and call on the jaguar's power to surround you with its protection.
4. Prepare yourself to accept the healing and protective love of the animal and to feel it with every part of your being.
5. Visualize the jaguar entering your energy field, protecting you, and keeping your energy safe from negative entities and unwanted energy.
6. Keep visualizing the jaguar and focus on it. Notice the way it moves with power, confidence, and grace.
7. The jaguar runs around you in circles, creating a protective shield and making you feel at peace because you know nothing can penetrate this shield.

8. End the meditation by giving thanks to the jaguar for its protection.

Energy Work

Energy work, also known as energy healing, is a practice that involves using Chi or energy life force to unblock your chakras and bring harmony, balance, and healing energy into your life. Energy work includes various techniques like tapping, massage, breathing exercises, healing crystals, reflexology, acupuncture, light therapy, reiki, and smudging. You can practice Some of these techniques while others, like acupuncture and reiki, require a professional.

Breathwork
Instructions:
1. Sit in a comfortable position and place your right hand over your belly.
2. Feel your belly expand as you inhale and feel the air release from your belly, emptying it as you exhale.
3. Put your left hand over your ribs and take a long deep breath. Feel your ribs expand while softening your belly.
4. Move your left hand to your upper chest. Breathe in, feeling your chest broadening, your ribs expanding, and your belly softening.
5. Breathe out and let out all the negativity.
6. Repeat these steps three to 10 times before any smudging ritual.

Meditation with Crystals
Instructions:
1. Choose the right crystals for you (the next chapter will explain this process in detail).
2. Set an intention. Say something like, *"I intend to use this meditation to release negative energy and protect myself from psychic attacks."*
3. Play relaxing music to keep you calm.
4. Sit in a comfortable position and hold one crystal in your right hand and place the others around you. You can lie down if you prefer and place the crystals over your body.
5. Take slow and deep breaths.

6. Close your eyes and imagine the crystals radiating warm and protective light surrounding you and keeping you safe.
7. Sit with this feeling until you feel protected.

Spirit Guides

Spirit guides are energy entities that provide guidance and support. Every person has one, and if you haven't felt it, they just haven't connected with you yet. They are always nearby helping you even when you don't ask for it. They can send you messages through dreams, symbols, or strange situations that you may brush off as coincidences. If you connect with your spirit guide, you will be able to decipher the messages they send you.

Your spirit guide can be an angel, animal, bird, or deceased ancestor. It is powerful and can protect you against all types of psychic attacks. Connecting with them will make it easier to ask for their help whenever you need protection.

Connecting with Your Spirit Guide
Instructions:
1. Create a sacred space like building an altar, or simply choose an undisturbed room and cleanse it.
2. Set an intention to practice this technique to communicate with your spirit guide.
3. Close your eyes and ask your spirit guide to join you.
4. Take a few deep breaths and clear your mind. Only focus on your spirit guide.
5. Say, "*Welcome, my spirit guide; please give me a sign you are here.*"
6. You will hear a voice, see an image, smell a scent, or get a feeling when they are here. Keep an open mind, and you will pick up on something. This may not happen immediately, and you may need to repeat this technique a few times until you can successfully communicate with them.
7. Once you notice their presence, ask for their help to protect you against psychic attacks while performing a smudging ritual.
8. You can see an image of white light surrounding you and protecting you or simply feel protected. Your guide will show you

in some way that they are keeping you safe.
9. When you feel protected, thank your spirit guide for their assistance and slowly open your eyes.

Smudging

You can practice smudging techniques to protect yourself against psychic attack symptoms.

Instructions:
1. Burn sage in a metallic bowl.
2. Let it burn until it releases thick smoke.
3. Hold the sage and cleanse yourself, starting with your head and moving down to every part of your body.
4. Imagine the negative energy separating from you and the smoke protecting you.
5. Leave the sage to finish burning.

Common Challenges When Smudging

Some common challenges and obstacles can crop up when practicing smudging for psychic protection. You can't protect yourself unless you silence these thoughts and believe in the power of this ritual.

Skepticism from Others

Some of your family members or friends may think it's strange that you use smoke to protect yourself from psychic attacks. They can either mock you or be skeptical. Either way, you shouldn't care what others think. Love and respect them but understand that each person has their own beliefs. They probably believe in things you don't agree with, but you respect those differences, and they should also.

However, if their skepticism bothers you, you can show them the history of smudging and how it has been an effective method for psychic protection for centuries. You can also show them all the scientific research proving smoke has strong healing properties.

Whether they start to believe in smudging or not, remember you have nothing to prove to anyone.

Difficulties with Visualization

Visualization is a big part of psychic protection methods. However, this technique doesn't come easily to everyone. A few simple tips can

ignite your imagination so you can create images in your mind.
- If you struggle with visualizing a specific image, try to conjure an event from your past. Think of the sounds, smells, and feelings associated with it, and keep focusing on them until you see an image.
- Sometimes, a smell can easily bring an image to mind. For instance, the smell of your grandmother's cooking will make you picture her and her house. The sound of a school bell can conjure up images of your childhood friends.
- Use songs, images, scents, food, and even objects you can touch – something that reminds you of a person or an event in your life. Whenever an image appears in your head, press on your thumb. In time, this can become an anchor, something you use to get you in the zone to visualize.

Self-Doubt
- You may not believe in yourself or your abilities. You think you don't have it in you to protect yourself from psychic attacks. Believing in yourself comes from within; get to the bottom of the self-doubt issue to relinquish it.
- Try journaling. Think of why you are doubting yourself, and write down all thoughts and feelings that you experience. The more you write, the easier you will get to the source of your doubts.
- When you discover the source, ask yourself more questions, like are your doubts reasonable or if you can control the thoughts that hold you back.
- Self-doubt stems from negative thoughts. By now, you understand that these thoughts aren't based on anything real. In the case of psychic attacks, the negative thoughts you experience aren't yours. They are transferred to you from someone else. You can use all the information you have on negative thoughts to rid yourself of them. Once these thoughts go away, so will your self-doubt.

Psychic attacks are serious and can impact every aspect of your life. However, smudging and all the techniques in this chapter can protect you and keep you safe at all times.

Chapter 9: Crystals and Smudging

Crystals are beautiful, colorful, and powerful stones. They come from stardust, lava, minerals, and other natural resources. Crystals contain energy, and since every human being is made from energy, you can exchange your negative vibes with the crystals' positive energy.

The wisdom and knowledge of crystals often feel spiritual rather than earthly. Every crystal has its own unique properties and radiates vibes matching its environment. They can cleanse, heal, and purify your spirit, body, and physical space. Therefore, you can use them in a smudging ritual for their cleansing and healing properties.

Crystals Used in Smudging

Although there are over four thousand crystals in the world, each has its own functions and uses. The first part of the chapter will cover the most common crystals used in smudging and their spiritual properties.

Clear Quartz

Clear quartz crystal.
https://unsplash.com/photos/k65_6C4hu2E

The clear quartz crystal is a transparent stone that provides healing, connects with your seven chakras, and amplifies power by significantly increasing the energy you pour into it and strengthening the vibrations of other crystals as well. It also cleanses your energy and surroundings. It often comes from frozen waters, and it resembles pieces of ice and radiates cooling energy. Since ancient times, this stone has been associated with myth, mysticism, and magic.

This crystal provides spiritual growth by pushing you to look within and discover who you truly are. It also unblocks the chakras, allowing energy to follow easily in your body and cleanse your aura. The clear quartz is associated with the crown chakra located over the top of your head. This chakra connects you with the Divine, higher planes of existence, and all the endless possibilities in the universe. It can balance, store, or release energy and bring you wisdom and awareness.

Clear quartz can improve your mental clarity, stabilize your emotions, and bring focus to whatever you desire. You can also use it for meditation and during manifestation rituals. This crystal has protective properties and can enhance your psychic powers. It has the unique ability to open your eyes to your truth and the truth of the people in your life so you can understand yourself better and see every situation from a different and fresh perspective. It can also bring harmony to your personal life and environment and mental and emotional clarity as well.

For this reason, it is often referred to as "The Universal Crystal" since it can be used in many aspects, like channeling, protection, meditation, and manifestation, and it is one of the most powerful and effective healing stones.

Amethyst

Amethyst crystal.
Marie-Lan Taÿ Pamart, CC BY 4.0 <https://creativecommons.org/licenses/by/4.0>, via Wikimedia Commons
https://commons.wikimedia.org/wiki/File:Amethyst_Siberia_MNHN_Min%C3%A9ralogie.jpg

Amethyst is a beautiful purple crystal that radiates wisdom, calmness, and spiritual healing. It acts as a bridge that connects the physical world with the spiritual world, the Divine, and provides spiritual awakening. For centuries, this stone has been associated with spirituality, the crown chakra, and the third eye.

"Amethyst" is derived from the Greek word "*Amethystos*," meaning "non-intoxicated" because the ancient Greeks used to wear it for protection against the effect of intoxication. The crystal has always been connected with magic and myth. In ancient Greek and Roman mythology, it is believed that amethyst got its color from the tears of the god of wine.

The legend says that Amethyst was a young virgin girl who was treated badly by Dionysus/Bacchus (gods of wine in Greek and Roman mythology, respectively) whenever he was drunk. She couldn't take it anymore and begged Diana/Artemis (goddesses of hunting and wild animals in Roman and Greek mythology) to help make her pain stop. So, the goddess turned her into a white stone. When the god of wine found out what had happened, he cried over the crystal until it turned purple. Thanks to this legend, amethyst has long since been associated with mental clarity and contemplation.

Everyone has intuition. They just don't know how to use it. The amethyst crystal unblocks your third eye and brings your sixth sense to life. It also awakens your intuition and invites wisdom and imagination into your life. The crystal is also connected to the crown chakra that opens you up to receive messages from the divine and the universe. It protects you against negative energy, bad emotions, and black magic.

Amethyst has strong spiritual vibes that increase your awareness. It can bring you closer to your guardian angel and spiritual guides. It gives you knowledge and shows you that you are one with the universe. The stone can fill your heart with Divine love and spiritual wisdom and reminds you that you aren't alone in the world. It improves your psychic abilities and facilitates visions and out-of-body experiences, and alters your energy to raise its frequency.

Black Tourmaline

Black tourmaline.
Jan Helebrant, CC BY-SA 2.0 <https://creativecommons.org/licenses/by-sa/2.0>, via Wikimedia Commons https://commons.wikimedia.org/wiki/File:Schorl_black_tourmaline_-_NaFe2%2B3Al6(BO3)3Si6O18(OH)4_(28838960018).jpg

Black tourmaline is one of the strongest crystals to use against negative energy and bad emotions. Although tourmaline comes in different colors, none is as powerful as the black one. The crystal is associated with the Muladhara chakra, the first of the chakras that makes you feel grounded and safe in your environment. The stone protects you against psychic attacks and energy vampires (negative people who drain your energy, leaving you feeling tired) and raises your vibrations. Black tourmaline purifies your body and surroundings from negative energy and dark entities. It elevates your consciousness and puts you on the path of enlightenment. It teaches you how to live a life in the service of others so you can make a difference in the world.

Ancient cultures used black tourmaline for its protective properties since it soaks up all negativity and acts as a shield against harmful energy.

Don't let its dark color fool you. Black tourmaline can also bring light and clarity to your environment. When life gets tough, and you feel stuck in your situation, this crystal will radiate light and positive energy, bring the love of the universe into your heart, and elevate your spiritual consciousness. It connects you to higher forces, balances your chakras, and encourages spiritual healing. Black tourmaline wands have unique properties as they can channel powerful energy that transcends the physical world to provide healing. They can also release negative energy from your aura to allow positivity to flow through your being.

You can use black tourmaline in spiritual meditation as it can safely take you to the spiritual world. If you dream of this crystal, it's a warning against danger.

Selenite

Selenite crystal.
https://unsplash.com/photos/vxf-uurQ5rY

This pearly white crystal owes its name to Selene, the Greek goddess of the moon. This makes it one of the most spiritual stones. If you look at it, you will sense a calmness washing over you. Its soothing qualities come from its pale white color that looks and feels otherworldly. In ancient Greece, Selenite was favored by the goddesses because it brings spiritual healing, harmony, and protection to your mind, body, and physical space.

The crystal can increase your vibrations so you can receive and interpret meaningful messages from the universe. It can unblock your seven chakras to facilitate energy flow, protect you against negative energy and entities, and bring purity and peace to your heart and mind.

Although selenite can provide mental, physical, and emotional healing, its most powerful attributes are in the spiritual and metaphysical realms. It can cleanse your aura and connect you with your spirit guide and highest self. Working with this stone can enhance your psychic abilities, open you up to discover all levels of your consciousness, access your past lives so you can heal from traumatic events, connect you to the spirit and angel world, and show you the path to the Divine.

The stone can bring positivity into your life and reminds you that you are a child of God and a part of the universe who deserves to be happy.

It pushes you forward to become the best version of yourself. It clears your vision so you can discover your passion and goals. It eliminates negative thoughts leading you to talk about yourself and your goals using positive and powerful statements. You can use this crystal in smudging, scrying, meditation, and manifestation.

Rose Quartz

Rose Quartz crystal.
Bergminer, CC BY-SA 4.0 <https://creativecommons.org/licenses/by-sa/4.0>, via Wikimedia Commons https://commons.wikimedia.org/wiki/File:Rose_quartz_Spain.jpg

Rose quartz belongs to the same family as clear quartz. It radiates positive and tender emotions and has become a symbol of love for centuries. Its healing properties can bring harmony into your life; most people love keeping it near them. It is associated with the throat chakra and the heart chakra. It can heal conflict and trauma in all types of relationships, whether romantic or not.

This crystal can unblock your heart chakra to open it up to love, joy, and other positive emotions. It can bring balance to your life, connect you to the world around you and the people in your life, bring you comfort, and show you all the possibilities in life. Rose quartz is linked to the female energy of the goddesses, attracts peace and compassion to your aura, and empowers your spirit. Its healing properties can calm your soul, show you your true potential, and comfort your broken heart.

It releases negative emotions like hatred, resentment, fear, and anger to purify your soul and end your pain.

The stone connects your heart to the Earth and the universe, giving you the courage to love and express your emotions without fear. After experiencing the healing properties of rose quartz, you will feel like a new person. You will be kinder, more hopeful, and your faith in yourself and the world will be restored. The stone will remind you that the secret to happiness is to love the people in your life unconditionally without waiting for anything in return, and the universe will send the same kind of love your way. You will learn that all of God's creation should be cherished and treated with respect.

Rose quartz has a motherly and nurturing presence, which you can use for support during harsh times. Its warm energy can make you feel loved, protected, and content and make you believe that anything is possible. It pushes you to ask yourself tough questions to show you that the answers are often simpler than you think.

Citrine

Citrine crystal.
Rama, CC BY-SA 3.0 FR <https://creativecommons.org/licenses/by-sa/3.0/fr/deed.en>, via Wikimedia Commons https://commons.wikimedia.org/wiki/File:Citrine_quartz-AMGL_79477-P5030194-black.jpg

Citrine is another crystal that belongs to the quartz family. This yellow stone can bring light and sunshine into your life and remind you that brighter days are ahead of you. It is linked to the solar plexus chakra and the sacral chakra. It keeps you grounded and brings balance and stability into your life. The crystal can unblock the solar plexus chakra to empower you and make you feel that you can handle anything life throws your way.

This crystal opens up your sacral chakra and brings intimacy, passion, and creativity into your life. It can also protect you against negative energy, empower your spirit, and invite positivity into your heart. You will be able to smile through the pain because you know things will always get better.

Suppose you are sensitive or easily affected by negative energies and entities. In that case, citrine can act as a shield to protect you from harmful influences. It is an abundance crystal that you can use to manifest success, prosperity, wealth, and a variety of wonderful things. During family conflicts, citrine can calm you down so you can think clearly and prevent the situation from escalating.

It also awakens your psychic abilities to understand the information and signs the universe sends to you. For some people, it can guide them to astral projects. It can also align and cleanse your aura, bring light and clarity to it, and provide mental and emotional healing.

The stone enhances your connection with your higher self and the Divine. People commonly use it during rituals and meditation to keep them grounded and invite enlightenment and awareness.

Obsidian

Obsidian.

B. Domangue, CC BY-SA 4.0 <https://creativecommons.org/licenses/by-sa/4.0>, via Wikimedia Commons https://commons.wikimedia.org/wiki/File:Obsidian_-_Igneous_Rock.jpg

Obsidian is a powerful dark crystal that protects you against negative energy. Although it is a black stone, it shows you that you can see through the darkness to discover the truth. Its clear surface resembles a mirror reflecting a vision of the future. Some believe they can use its clear surface to awaken their higher consciousness.

The crystal is linked to the root chakra that keeps you grounded even if your world is turning upside down. Obsidian can unblock your root chakra, allowing for smooth energy flow, making you feel safe and strong, and protecting you against psychic attacks. Ancient cultures used this stone to awaken the third eye chakra and to visit the spiritual world.

Each person has a dark side that they aren't usually aware of. Obsidian reveals this side to you to show you a different side of your personality. It uncovers your strengths, weaknesses, capabilities, and even parts of yourself that you have forgotten. The crystal gives your soul a purpose, enhances spiritual growth, and pushes you to explore the mysteries of the universe.

The stones align your spirit with your mind and body, release negative energy, and invite harmony and peace into your life.

Methods of Incorporating Crystals into a Smudging Practice

This part of the chapter will focus on the different ways you can use crystals in your smudging rituals.

Placing Crystals around the Space

Before smudging, placing crystals around the space amplifies the energy and supports the cleansing process. Good crystals for this purpose include clear quartz, amethyst, black tourmaline, and selenite.

You can also create a crystal grid by arranging the stones into a sacred geometric position to strengthen their energy. There are various grids you can find online, or you can use grid cloths.

Crystal Wand

Use a crystal wand to direct the smoke from the smudge stick. Choose one that fits your intentions or needs (a clear quartz wand for amplifying energy or a rose quartz wand for love and healing). You can choose a crystal wand by holding it in your hand. If you connect with it immediately, it is the right stone for you. If you shop online, you can use the information here to guide you.

Ask yourself why you are performing this ritual. Do you want to cleanse your surroundings? Do you want to protect yourself against negative energy? Or do you want to amplify the energy of an object? Your answers will determine which crystal to use.

Build a Crystal Altar

Build an altar and add one or more crystals to it. You can perform smudging rituals at the altar to harness the stones' energy.

Holding Crystals

Holding crystals while smudging infuses them with cleansing energy and helps them focus on your intentions.

To set your intention, follow these simple instructions:

1. Hold the stone with your dominant hand.
2. Close your eyes and clear your mind.
3. Take a few deep and slow breaths until you feel grounded.

4. Imagine yourself standing in nature, taking in the beautiful scenery and feeling calm and relaxed.
5. Imagine there is a large version of the crystal right before you.
6. Step inside the crystal to explore it. Visualize every part of the inside of the crystal, like its scent, look, sound, and the feeling you experience at this moment. Everything should look and feel real.
7. Now focus on your intention and fill the inside of the crystal with people, colors, symbols, objects, etc., associated with your goal and what you hope to achieve from this ritual.
8. After adding the final touches, sit, and take in your surroundings.
9. When you feel comfortable, repeat your intention out loud in real life and in the visualization.
10. Imagine yourself carving or writing every word of your intention on the inside walls of your crystal.
11. Sit in your crystal for a while. Walk around and study every part of it. Spread positive every all around.
12. You can now use it in your ritual.

Charging/Programming Crystals with Smoke

After smudging, hold crystals in the smoke to cleanse and charge them. This can help to reset their energy and enhance their healing properties. Remember, there is negative energy all around you. During the ritual, your crystals can absorb this energy, affecting your surroundings and ruining your next ritual. Cleansing the crystals will release all the bad energy and entities, charging your crystal with loving and positive vibes.

Instructions:

1. Pass your crystal over the smoke for a couple of minutes.
2. Set an intention to charge your crystal with positive energy and release negative energy.

Crystals are extremely powerful and can amplify the energy and healing properties during any smudging rituals. Before choosing a stone, study its spiritual and healing properties to find the one that fits your needs. When buying a crystal, don't just take the first one you see. Let the right one call out to you. Keep an open mind, and let your heart guide you. You will often establish a connection with your crystal right away. Once you choose, cleanse it using smoke and infuse it with your intention and positive energy. In a short time, you will begin to notice the powerful impact of these enchanting stones on your ritual.

Chapter 10: Healing with Smudging

Throughout the book, you will have encountered several instances showing the power of healing through smudging. And suppose you have already tried some of the techniques before reaching this point. In that case, you may have experienced its restorative properties for yourself. Indeed, one of the lesser-known secrets of smudging is its capacity to heal numerous ailments, not just physical diseases but spiritual and emotional maladies as well.

Healing Physical Diseases

Studies have shown that sage, the herb most commonly used for smudging, has antibacterial and antimicrobial properties. In its natural environment, sage is known to repel some of the most harmful insects as well. Did you know that the herb is an antioxidant that can eliminate over 90% of bacteria in a room?

Here's another interesting fact: sage is called *salvia* in Latin, and *salvia*'s linguistic roots can be traced to the word *heal* (Harry Potter fans might know the spell *salvio hexia*, used to repel physically harmful hexes). Burning sage can boost your immunity and protect you from various diseases.

The other herbs used in smudging rituals also contain several physical healing properties.

- **Cedar**

Like sage, cedar also repels insects. If you inhale the cedar smoke generated by smudging, it will open up your air pipes, allowing you to breathe more freely while helping you take care of any existing respiratory diseases. And are you often prone to arthritis? Cedar smudging may help ease the pain and reduce the inflammation in your joints.

- **Palo Santo**

The smoke from palo santo smudging may cure several respiratory ailments like asthma. Its wood oil may be used to cure arthritis, and it may even improve your skin health. Research suggests that the d-limonene compound found in palo santo wood may help protect you from cancer.

- **Sweetgrass**

The smoke from burning sweetgrass is known to heal the common cold. If you make tea out of this plant, it may even cure your incessant coughs and fever. The oil from sweetgrass may heal your wounds by its virtue of repelling bacteria.

- **Lavender**

Over the years, lavender smoke has been used to relieve headaches and migraines. It is possible to reduce joint inflammation and alleviate muscle aches with the plant. Its antibacterial properties may help cure eczema. Additionally, lavender smudging improves both blood and air circulation in your body.

- **Frankincense and Myrrh**

Studies have repeatedly shown that smudging with frankincense and myrrh can kill harmful airborne bacteria. It is said that inhaled smoke can create white blood cells in your body, thus boosting your immunity to several diseases. Frankincense and myrrh also have anti-inflammatory properties and can even aid in getting rid of skin problems.

It goes without saying that no matter which herb, resin, or oil you use for smudging, some or the other of your physical ailments will most probably be healed. It may be a persistent skin rash, chronic sinusitis, recurring migraines, or even something as fatal as cancer.

Healing Spiritual Illnesses

Experts believe that physical diseases can trace their roots to your energy body. If harmful bacteria enter your system, their degrading effects are first apparent in your energy body before they affect your physical body. These effects are called spiritual illnesses, and they must be eliminated before you can be physically cured. That is exactly what smudging is most capable of doing.

The smudging process can detect the spiritual cause of your physical problems and wrench it out of your system before it causes your health to deteriorate any further. The negative energies present in your energy body are removed, leaving it ready and open to be filled with a burst of positive energy, healing all your spiritual illnesses. In short, smudging purifies your spirit, cleanses your energy, and heals your soul. It can cure illnesses by getting rid of the root cause. These causes include,

- **Ancestral Spirits**

Did you recently make some of your ancestors unhappy? Did you do something that they would not have approved of? Then they might have cursed you with a physical disease you are currently suffering from. Smudging clears the negative energy from your ancestral spirits, bringing happiness back into their souls and curing you of the disease.

- **Household Spirits**

Did you fail to follow the teachings of your household spirit? Your actions may have enraged that deity who, in turn, may have brought about some misfortune on your energy body. Smudging can eliminate that spiritual anger, cleansing and healing your energy body.

- **Harmful/Evil Spirits**

There is a possibility that certain harmful spirits are circling you or your space, negatively affecting your spirit. Smudging can either remove the evilness from the spirits or eliminate them altogether. Either way, your spiritual health will be immensely improved.

- **Soul Loss**

This is probably the worst spiritual illness you can experience. It implies what it states; the loss of your soul. Have you experienced some loss in real life? Maybe your loved one passed away, or you were the victim of an assault or an accident? Each real-life loss is believed to break the soul into fragments, eventually leading to complete soul loss (which leads to fatal, incurable diseases). Smudging heals your soul, mending each fragment and making it whole.

As you can see, your spiritual health directly affects your physical well-being. The purer your energy body, the better will your physical state be. And the process of smudging heals both bodies!

Healing Emotional Disorders

This is the most important and highly effective impact of smudging. As you might know by now, smudging focuses on removing the negative energy from a space or a person. And more often than not, that negative energy is created due to your negative emotions. Thus, it can be safely concluded that smudging heals emotional disorders from a space or a person. Indeed, emotional harmony is the smudging process's most conspicuous, immediately apparent result.

- **Anxiety**

As healing emotional disorders is similar to all other types of physical healing, healing anxiety is similar to healing all other types of emotional disorders. As soon as you complete any of the smudging techniques, the first thing you will notice in yourself is the absolute lack of anxiety. It will be replaced by serenity so profound that all your other problems will seem to vanish into thin air (the problems may still be there, you just won't feel anxious about them).

- **Stress**

On the surface, stress may seem no different from anxiety. After all, you feel anxious when stressed, and vice versa. But they are responses to entirely different situations. Anxiety is more of a fear of things that haven't yet happened, whereas stress is the pressure you feel about things you're currently experiencing. You can say that stress is a milder form of anxiety, but it can overwhelm and crush you if felt in excess.

The soothing fumes surrounding you after smudging help reduce that stress, and the expunged negative energy wipes out the remaining pressure from your mind. You will start to think more clearly and manage your work and personal life more efficiently.

- **Depression**

This is one of the deadliest kinds of negative emotions. It can be fatal if left unchecked (leading to clinical depression). Unlike anxiety or stress, where you know outside factors are negatively affecting you, depression creeps up in complete secrecy, and, in this case, you are the one who is destroying your emotional state (no outside factors whatsoever).

When you are depressed, the negative energy almost always lies within you, not in the space around you or within other people. Smudging can help drive that energy out of you, expelling even those negative emotions that make you depressed.

- **Anger**

In a disturbed mind, anger is the most commonly felt emotion. Whenever you are nervous or stressed, you are often quick to feel anger. That is when the calming presence of smudging techniques shines best. The comforting smoke that wafts throughout the room enters your energy body and pushes out the anger-inducing negative emotions, creating a sense of peace within your soul. You may remember what you were angry about at the end of the process, but the situation won't allow you to feel that anger.

- **Hatred**

You may be feeling absolute, unrestrained hatred toward a person or a situation, so fiery and all-consuming that you may not feel love for anyone or anything else. Deep, intense hatred like this can be removed through smudging. At the end of the ritual, the state of oneness that you reach will help you forgive and forget the hatred for that person or place, replacing it with either apathy or love.

Other negative emotions, like guilt, frustration, jealousy, boredom, etc., can also be healed via smudging. Once the rituals are complete, you will reach an emotional balance with positive and negative emotions in equal measure, giving rise to a state of absolute calm. And if you look closely at the healing of emotions through smudging, you will realize that your emotional health depends on the strength of your spirit, which in turn depends on your physical well-being (and vice versa). It's all interconnected!

How to Heal with Smudging

The processes, techniques, and rituals of smudging remain the same, as detailed in the book's earlier sections. The only thing that changes is your *focus*. So far, you have been focusing on the general aspects of smudging, like believing that the negative energy in a space or within yourself is leaving. This time, you will need to focus on one form of negative energy during the smudging process.

Imagine that you wish to get rid of your anger. While beginning the smudging ritual and burning the herb, focus on pushing that anger out of your system. Concentrate on the chakras connected to anger (the one near the base of your spine and the other just above your navel) and believe they are being purified. That is how your anger will eventually subside into a sense of serenity.

In your astral/energy body, the chakras associated with emotions and diseases are,

1. **Root Chakra**

    Diseases: Arthritis, colon issues, constipation.

    Negative emotions: Anger, instability, fear, frustration.

2. **Sacral Chakra**

    Diseases: Lack of sexual drive, urinary tract problems, lower back issues.

    Negative emotions: Irritability, lethargy, manipulative tendencies.

3. **Solar Plexus Chakra**

    Diseases: Indigestion, diabetes, liver issues.

    Negative emotions: Low self-esteem, depression, rage.

4. **Heart Chakra**

    Diseases: Heart issues, weight instability, asthma.

    Negative emotions: Jealousy, dread, anxiety.

5. **Throat Chakra**

    Diseases: Thyroid problems, dental anomalies, breathing issues.

    Negative emotions: Inability to express your thoughts, introvert.

6. **Third Eye Chakra**

    Diseases: Headaches, migraines, hearing troubles, blindness.

    Negative emotions: Fear of success, selfishness.

7. **Crown Chakra**

    Diseases: Mental illnesses, nervous system imbalances.

    Negative emotions: Frustration, skepticism, suicidal tendencies.

You need to be at one with your energy body to be able to focus on your chakras. Each chakra should be clearly visible in your mind's eye; otherwise, this technique won't always work. That said, focusing on purifying your chakras is only one of the many healing methods with smudging.

- **Meditation**

Meditation literally means to focus on something for a set amount of time. You will need to clear your mind of all thoughts but one. For healing purposes, that thought should be part of your body, the type of spirit, or the kind of emotion you are trying to heal with smudging.

Another important part of meditation is your breathing. It should be slow and rhythmic. Breathe in, hold for a few seconds, breathe out, hold again, and repeat the process. A point to note: you must be experienced at smudging to heal using meditation techniques. That is because you don't want to be thinking about the ritual itself to make meditation successful. The acts of the ritual should be spontaneous, instinctual, and only one thought of healing should rule your state of mind.

- **Visualization**

This is almost the same as meditation. With visualization, you need to create a picture of the part of your body, spirit, or emotion you wish to heal. Thinking about it is one thing, but here, you need to believe that the part is actually in front of you. You can see it in your mind's eye, reach out for it and feel it. Let this feeling envelop your soul until you see nothing but the part to be healed. The smudging process will take care of the rest.

Consider that you wish to heal your diabetes. Begin the smudging ritual and visualize the diabetes in your body. Conjure up an image of the interior of your physical body. Imagine the blood flowing through your veins, as red as a beet in the sunshine. Now visualize the glucose as small yellow dots sprinkled throughout the bloodstream, like patches of weed on an otherwise fresh field. Finally, realize that the dots are diminishing, leaving your bloodstream.

Repeat this process during every one of your smudging rituals.

- **Prayer**

It is said that words are as powerful as visuals, and sometimes, they can move you more than an image ever could. And prayer can do wonders when you are using smudging to heal. It doesn't matter if it is a long, complex prayer suggested by a trusted shaman or a short, simple combination of words of your own making. What matters here is your understanding of that prayer and your belief in the words uttered. The stronger your belief, the more effective the ritual will be.

Assume that you wish to heal the suffering of your ancestral spirits. Let's say you have wronged them by taking your family business in a direction they don't like. In your prayer, start with an apology followed by an explanation, and end with a plea for forgiveness. It could go something like this,

"O ancestral spirits (name them if you want), I'm sorry for my actions, but it was the best solution to find success in these trying times. Forgive me if you can."

Feel free to be more creative or even make poetry out of it. As long as you believe in the words and focus on bringing them to fruition, you can even sing them out loud! For healing, all that matters is your focus.

The Science Behind Healing with Smudging

You heard it right. Smudging is supported by science! The most fundamental science behind the ritual is that the smoke generated by smudging repels harmful bacteria from the environment. Studies have shown that more than 90% of bacteria is removed. Also, the smoke is easily absorbed into your system, reinvigorating your brain and bodily functions. Unlike tobacco smoke with a lethargic effect, the medicinal smoke of sage, cedar, or any other herbs makes you lively and energetic, ready to take on the world. The science behind that is the presence of negative ions in the smoke.

Don't worry! Negative ions aren't negative in the philosophical sense. When your body contains negative energy, it gets filled with positive ions (which are emotionally harmful). The negative ions released from the smudge smoke get absorbed into your body, canceling out the effect of the positive ions and opening up a door for positive energy to enter.

Smudging to Heal and Improve Holistic Health

Holistic health implies your overall health, including its physical, emotional, spiritual, intellectual, and social aspects. So far, you have learned how smudging can heal your physical, emotional, and spiritual being. Did you know that it can also rejuvenate the intellectual and social parts of your life?

When negative energy is removed from you and your space, your mind will be cleansed. This cleansing will allow you to analyze things objectively and heighten your faculty of reasoning. And that is exactly what a high level of intellect is! With this renewed clarity of knowledge, you can fill your cleansed mind with positive energy.

As you might have surmised, your social health depends on the kind of relationship you have developed with the people around you. Your social health is good if it is full of love and happiness. But your social health needs major improvements if it is rife with bickering and hostility. Smudging can heal your social life by removing the negative energy and emotions from your surroundings, yourself, and the surroundings and souls of your acquaintances, friends, and family.

In essence, smudging can heal your holistic health to improve your overall well-being. You can easily incorporate it into your daily wellness routine. Any time of the day or night is perfect for conducting the ritual. All that matters is your willingness to let go of the negative energy and your enthusiasm to invite positivity into your life.

Conclusion

Imagine this: After a long, exhausting day, you walk into your home, light up some sage, and let the fragrant smoke waft through the air. It's like a breath of fresh air, washing away all the stress and negative vibes that cling to you. Suddenly, your space feels lighter, calmer, and more inviting. It's as if smudging gives you a reset button, allowing you to leave behind the chaos and find a sense of peace within your surroundings. But smudging goes beyond creating a cozy atmosphere. It can also be a guiding light during times of change and transition. Smudging can be your faithful companion, whether moving to a new home, starting a new job, or going through a significant life change. It's like having a trusted friend who helps you let go of the past and embrace the possibilities of the future. With each swirl of the sacred smoke, you create a clean slate, inviting positive energy and new beginnings into your life.

And let's not forget about the spiritual side of smudging. It's like you have a direct line to your inner self and the greater universe. You're setting the stage for deep connection and self-discovery when you smudge before meditation, prayer, or any soul-searching practice. The gentle tendrils of smoke bridge the gap between the physical and the spiritual, helping you find a sense of harmony and unity within yourself. The best part? Smudging isn't just for spaces and rituals. It's adaptable to various situations. You can use it to cleanse and revitalize your cherished objects, such as your favorite crystals or sentimental jewelry, giving them a rejuvenating spa treatment, clearing away any lingering negative energy, and recharging them with positivity. And why not smudge yourself too? It will feel like you have a mini self-care routine for your energy field, allowing you to shed any heaviness and embrace renewed vitality.

So, as you close this book and end your exploration of smudging practices, remember this. It's not just a one-off practice; it's a way of life. It's about integrating smudging into your daily routine, like that cup of tea that brings you comfort and warmth each morning. By embracing the transformative power of smudging, you invite harmony, peace, and positive energy into your life. So go ahead, start smudging, and watch the magic unfold.

Here's another book by Mari Silva that you might like

Your Free Gift
(only available for a limited time)

Thanks for getting this book! If you want to learn more about various spirituality topics, then join Mari Silva's community and get a free guided meditation MP3 for awakening your third eye. This guided meditation mp3 is designed to open and strengthen ones third eye so you can experience a higher state of consciousness. Simply visit the link below the image to get started.

https://spiritualityspot.com/meditation

Or, Scan the QR code!

References

(N.d.). A-z-animals.com. https://a-z-animals.com/blog/jaguar-spirit-animal-symbolism-meaning/#:~:text=The%20jaguar%20is%20a%20symbol,intuition%2C%20confidence%2C%20and%20decisiveness

8 Reasons You Should Try Smudging & How To Do It At Home. (2017, May 8). Natural Living Ideas. https://www.naturallivingideas.com/smudging/

About sacred herbs & smudging ceremonies. (n.d.). Taosherb.com. https://www.taosherb.com/store/sacred-herbs.html

Acevedo, A. (2022, May 12). What is energy (as it relates to the law of attraction)? We explain. YouAlignedTM. https://youaligned.com/wellness/what-is-energy/

Amethyst - metaphysical healing properties. (n.d.). CRYSTALS & HOLISTIC HEALING. https://www.healingwithcrystals.net.au/amethyst.html

Amethyst meaning: Everything you NEED to know - healing properties & everyday uses. (n.d.). Tiny Rituals. https://tinyrituals.co/blogs/tiny-rituals/amethyst-meaning-healing-properties-and-everyday-uses

Askinosie, H. (2016, February 5). 8 ways to use crystals in your everyday routine. Mindbodygreen. https://www.mindbodygreen.com/articles/how-to-use-crystals-everyday

Ausler, N. (2022, December 4). 10 signs you're under A psychic attack & someone is sending you bad energy. YourTango. https://www.yourtango.com/self/signs-psychic-attack

Bauer, S. (2020, December 15). 10 of the incredible benefits of Palo Santo. Palo Santo Supply Company Ltd. https://palosantosupply.co/blogs/palo-santo/5-of-the-incredible-benefits-of-palo-santo

Beaulieu, C. (2022, August 13). 9 effective ways to protect yourself from psychic attacks. The Friendly Specter. https://www.friendlyspecter.com/9-effective-ways-to-protect-yourself-from-psychic-attacks/

Behind the meaning. (n.d.). Daisy London. https://www.daisyjewellery.com/blogs/our-world/behind-the-meaning-the-crown-chakra

Biancuzzo, M. (2022, April 5). 5 easy tips to help if you have trouble visualizing. Marie Biancuzzo, RN MS CCL IBCLC; MarieBiancuzzo.com. https://mariebiancuzzo.com/2022/04/05/5-easy-tips-to-help-if-you-have-trouble-visualizing/

Bihl, E. (2019, January 7). How to Smudge the Right Way (and Why You Should Do It). Brit + Co. https://www.brit.co/sage-smudging-tips/

Black Tourmaline Meaning: Healing properties & everyday uses. (n.d.). Tiny Rituals. https://tinyrituals.co/blogs/tiny-rituals/black-tourmaline-meaning-healing-properties-and-everyday-uses

Black Tourmaline. (2009). In Dictionary of Gems and Gemology (pp. 93–93). Springer Berlin Heidelberg.

Black Tourmaline: Meaning, healing properties, and powers. (n.d.). Mycrystals.com. https://www.mycrystals.com/meaning/black-tourmaline-meaning-healing-properties-and-powers

Bobb, B. (2022, August 10). Does burning sage really help you energetically cleanse your space? Vogue India. https://www.vogue.in/beauty/content/does-burning-sage-really-help-you-energetically-cleanse-your-space

Bolt, L. (2021, August 13). What is a spirit guide? Spirit guide meaning & more. Yahoo Life. https://www.yahoo.com/lifestyle/spirit-guide-spirit-guide-meaning-031900227.html

Bradford, D. (2023, January 1). How To Smudge Your House With Sage. Angels and Sages. https://angelsandsages.com/blogs/news/how-to-smudge-your-house-with-sage

Caron, A. (2021, September 23). Learn how to smudge. Seven Generations Education Institute. https://www.7generations.org/learn-how-to-smudge/

Chinnaiyan, K. (2017, February 23). 3 causes of self-doubt and how to conquer it for good. Tiny Buddha. https://tinybuddha.com/blog/3-causes-self-doubt-conquer-good/

Cho, A. (2012, July 7). Clear quartz meaning, healing properties, & uses. The Spruce. https://www.thespruce.com/what-is-a-clear-quartz-crystal-1274383

Cho, A. (n.d.). How to Smudge Your House to Invite Positive Energy. The Spruce. https://www.thespruce.com/how-to-smudge-your-house-1274692

Citrine - metaphysical healing properties. (n.d.). CRYSTALS & HOLISTIC HEALING. https://www.healingwithcrystals.net.au/citrine.html

Citrine meaning: Healing properties & everyday uses. (n.d.). Tiny Rituals. https://tinyrituals.co/blogs/tiny-rituals/citrine-meaning-healing-properties

Clear Quartz Meaning: Healing Properties & Uses. (n.d.). Tiny Rituals. https://tinyrituals.co/blogs/tiny-rituals/clear-quartz-meaning-healing-properties-uses

Coach, C. H. T. (1516444334000). Smudging - The science behind it. Linkedin.com. https://www.linkedin.com/pulse/smudging-science-behind-charmaine-howard

Dellner, A. (2018, April 26). What is energy work (and should I try it)? PureWow. https://www.purewow.com/wellness/energy-work

Detchon, A. (1528710839000). The importance of grounding and protecting your energy. Linkedin.com. https://www.linkedin.com/pulse/importance-grounding-protecting-your-energy-andrea-detchon-bsc-/

Dignity health. (n.d.). Dignity-Health. https://www.dignityhealth.org/articles/what-is-holistic-health-care-anyway

Dimensions of wellness. (n.d.). Rwu.edu. https://www.rwu.edu/undergraduate/student-life/health-and-counseling/health-education-program/dimensions-wellness

Energetic Harmony, let all your energy flow the right way. (n.d.). Attunements. https://www.attunements.info/product/energetic-harmony/

Ferraro, K. (2022, December 31). 10 Easy Ways To Cleanse Your Home of Negative Energy. Mindbodygreen. https://www.mindbodygreen.com/articles/how-to-cleanse-your-home-of-negative-energy

Five steps to deepen your relationship with your spirit guide. (n.d.). Kripalu. https://kripalu.org/resources/five-steps-deepen-your-relationship-your-spirit-guide

Frankincense incense benefits: 12 crucial things to know. (n.d.). Tiny Rituals. https://tinyrituals.co/blogs/tiny-rituals/frankincense-incense-benefits

Gemstone information - quartz Crystal Meaning and properties - fire mountain gems and beads. (n.d.). Firemountaingems.com. https://www.firemountaingems.com/resources/encyclobeadia/gem-notes/gmstnprprtsrckc

Graham, M. (2020, May 21). Benefits of Smudging with Sage (5 Scientific Reasons to SMUDGE with Sage!). Tribal Trade. https://tribaltradeco.com/blogs/smudging/benefits-of-smudging-with-sage-5-scientific-reasons-to-smudge-with-sage

Hannah, R. (1422379428000). What is A psychic attack? Linkedin.com. https://www.linkedin.com/pulse/what-psychic-attack-raven-hannah/

How crystals can help you stay connected to your intentions. (2016, March 31). Mindbodygreen. https://www.mindbodygreen.com/articles/intention-setting-with-gemstones-crystals

How to Choose which Crystal is right for you ? (n.d.). Wands of Lust Co. https://www.wandsoflust.com.au/blogs/news/how-to-choose-which-crystal-is-right-for-you

How to know if your crystals need charging + 9 potent methods. (2021, June 15). Mindbodygreen. https://www.mindbodygreen.com/articles/how-to-charge-crystals

How to make a DIY sage smudge stick. (n.d.). Rise Gardens. https://risegardens.com/blogs/communitygarden/how-to-make-a-diy-sage-smudge-stick

Hurst, M. (2023, April 25). "Sound cleansing" – the easiest, most calming way to show negative energy the door. Homesandgardens.Com; Homes & Gardens. https://www.homesandgardens.com/life-design/sound-cleansing

Ibe, O. (2022, March 31). Earthing–A technique to help ground your body. Verywell Mind. https://www.verywellmind.com/what-is-earthing-5220089

Jain, R. (2020, October 8). Crown Chakra: Discover the divine energy of Sahasrara chakra. Arhanta Yoga Ashrams. https://www.arhantayoga.org/blog/crown-chakra-divine-energy-of-sahasrara-chakra/

Jay, S. (2022, August 3). 6 Cleansing Rituals For You & Your Home. Revoloon. https://revoloon.com/shanijay/cleansing-ritual

Jones, L. (2023, January 28). 35 grounding techniques for upsetting thoughts. Claritytherapynyc.com. https://www.claritytherapynyc.com/35-grounding-techniques-for-upsetting-thoughts/

Joseph, B. (2017, February 16). A Definition of Smudging. Ictinc.Ca. https://www.ictinc.ca/blog/a-definition-of-smudging

Julie. (2022a, February 5). Black Tourmaline meaning. Moonrise Crystals. https://moonrisecrystals.com/black-tourmaline-meaning/

Julie. (2022b, February 5). Selenite meaning. Moonrise Crystals. https://moonrisecrystals.com/selenite-meaning/

Julie. (2022c, February 6). Rose Quartz meaning. Moonrise Crystals. https://moonrisecrystals.com/rose-quartz-meaning/

Kyla. (2022, July 19). Aura Cleansing Spray – DIY Sage Spray for Spiritual Cleansing + Protection. A Life Adjacent. https://alifeadjacent.com/aura-cleansing-spray/

Lagman, R. (2021, July 13). Smudge prayer examples - part II: What to say when you're smudging to get rid of spiritual energy. Tribal Trade. https://tribaltradeco.com/blogs/teachings/smudge-prayer-examples-part-ii-what-to-say-when-you-re-smudging-to-get-rid-of-spiritual-energy

Lashi, B. (n.d.). Life Organic Blog [Organic Beauty/Minimalism/Wellness]. Embodyzen.Com. https://www.embodyzen.com/blog/8-step-smoke-bathing-ritual

Lim, E. (2021, November 6). How to create a personal energy shield for protection via visualisation. ILLUMINATION. https://medium.com/illumination/how-to-create-a-personal-energy-shield-for-protection-via-visualisation-23c8af69be56

Loewe, E. (2021, June 24). 5 Spiritual Smudge Sprays That Are Sustainable Or Indigenous-Made. Mindbodygreen. https://www.mindbodygreen.com/articles/smudge-sprays-what-they-are-4-to-start-with

M., X. (2020, April 2). Smudging for Healing. Villagerockshop.com. https://www.villagerockshop.com/blog/smudging-for-healing/

Maclean, L. (2021, March 22). 7 signs you're under psychic attack & how to stop it (2023). Mysticmag.com; MysticMag. https://www.mysticmag.com/psychic-reading/3-signs-youre-under-psychic-attack/

Majsiak, B., Young, C., & Laube, J. (n.d.). A beginner's guide to breath work practices. Everydayhealth.com. https://www.everydayhealth.com/alternative-health/living-with/ways-practice-breath-focused-meditation/

Marci. (n.d.). Smudge Prayer to Invoke the Four Directions. Marci Cagen. https://marcicagen.com/smudge-prayer-to-invoke-the-four-directions/

McKnight, J. (2020, December 5). 3 effective empath shielding meditations. Planet Meditate. https://planetmeditate.com/empath-shielding-meditation/

McQuerry, L. (n.d.). Make your own Smudge Stick. Moon Magic Co. https://moonmagic.co/blogs/news/make-your-own-smudge-stick

Morning, J. (2021, November 15). What is grounding, and how can it help me? Spunout. https://spunout.ie/mental-health/self-care/what-is-grounding

Natural essential oil pure blend smudging sage - island essentials: Natural body & hair care products. (2021, July 12). Island Essentials: Natural Body & Hair Care Products - Natural Body & Hair Care; Island Essentials. https://islandessentials.ca/shop/island-essentials/essential-oils-carrier-oils/essential-oils/essential-oil-blends/natural-essential-oil-pure-blend-smudging-sage/

Nesci, N. (2020, March 4). *5 things everyone needs to know about energy healing*. The Growth & Wellness Therapy Centre. https://www.growthwellnesstherapy.com/our-blog/5-things-everyone-needs-to-know-about-energy-healing

No title. (n.d.). Pranaworld.net. https://pranaworld.net/what-is-the-energy-body/

O'Connor, B. (2015, November 23). *7 sacred resins to burn for clearing negative....* Spirituality+Health. https://www.spiritualityhealth.com/blogs/your-creative-spirit/2015/11/23/bess-oconnor-7-sacred-resins-burn-clearing-negative-energy

Obsidian – metaphysical healing properties. (n.d.). CRYSTALS & HOLISTIC HEALING. https://www.healingwithcrystals.net.au/obsidian.html

Obsidian meaning. (n.d.). Anahana.com. https://www.anahana.com/en/lifestyle/crystals/obsidian-meaning

Obsidian meaning: Healing properties & everyday uses. (n.d.). Tiny Rituals. https://tinyrituals.co/blogs/tiny-rituals/obsidian-meaning-healing-properties-everyday-uses

Ohren, K. (2021a, August 8). *Citrine healing properties, meanings, and uses.* Crystal Vaults. https://www.crystalvaults.com/crystal-encyclopedia/citrine/

Ohren, K. (2021b, August 11). *Black Tourmaline healing properties, meanings, and uses.* Crystal Vaults. https://www.crystalvaults.com/crystal-encyclopedia/black-tourmaline/

Page, K., & Jane, P. (2017, December 9). *30 sacred herbs for smudging and cleansing purposes.* Ilmylunajane. https://www.ilmylunajane.com/single-post/2017/12/09/30-sacred-herbs-for-smudging-and-cleansing-purposes

Pollard, S. (2020, October 13). *Make your own smudge sticks to banish bad energy.* Hello Nest. https://hellonest.co/diy-smudge-sticks/

Pollard, S. (2022, January 12). *How to make your own Rosemary sage Smudge Sticks.* Hello Glow. https://helloglow.co/how-to-make-your-own-rosemary-sage-smudge-sticks/

Proctor, B. (2022, April 11). *The law of attraction vs. The law of vibration.* Proctor Gallagher Institute. https://www.proctorgallagherinstitute.com/47878/the-law-of-attraction-vs-the-law-of-vibration

Regan, S. (2022, April 26). *How To Make Your Bath A Spiritual Experience: 16 Tips & Techniques.* Mindbodygreen. https://www.mindbodygreen.com/articles/spiritual-bath

Regan, S. (2023, May 10). *How Sound Baths Are Revolutionizing Healing + How To Try One For Yourself.* Mindbodygreen. https://www.mindbodygreen.com/articles/sound-bath

Rekstis, E. (2022, November 15). Healing Crystals 101: Everything you need to know.

Ress, J. (2019, March 29). How To Use the Healing Powers of Quartz Crystals. SpaGoddess Apothecary. https://spagoddess.com/blogs/spagoddess-wellness-blog/clear-quartz-crystals

Richards, D. (2000). Rose Quartz. Daphne Richards.

Robby. (2021, February 27). The Benefits of Smudging: Why It's an Ancient Tradition. Dr. Lam Coaching – World Renowned Authority on Adrenal Fatigue Recovery. https://www.drlamcoaching.com/blog/benefits-of-smudging/

Rooted Revival. (2023, April 10). 9 sensational cedar smudge stick benefits. Rooted Revival. https://rootedrevival.com/cedar-smudge-stick-benefits/

Rooted Revival. (2023, June 9). 12 fantastic lavender smudge stick benefits. Rooted Revival. https://rootedrevival.com/lavender-smudge-stick-benefits/

Rose Quartz Meaning: Healing properties and everyday uses. (n.d.). Tiny Rituals. https://tinyrituals.co/blogs/tiny-rituals/rose-quartz-meaning-healing-properties-and-everyday-uses

Rose quartz: Meaning, healing properties and powers. (n.d.). Mycrystals.com. https://www.mycrystals.com/meaning/rose-quartz-meaning-and-healing-properties

Ryan, K. (2019, April 29). Supercharge: What you need to know about cleansing crystals. Wanderlust. https://wanderlust.com/journal/supercharge-what-you-need-to-know-about-cleansing-crystals/

Sake, F. P. (2017, September 12). Thirteen Quick Ways to Cleanse Energy. For Puck's Sake. https://www.patheos.com/blogs/matauryn/2017/09/12/thirteen-quick-energy-cleanse/

Salt Water Bath: A Cleansing, Healing, And Nourishing Ritual For Your Mind And Body. (n.d.). Linkedin.Com. https://www.linkedin.com/pulse/salt-water-bath-cleansing-healing-nourishing-ritual-your-mind-/

Salzberg, S. (2022, November 14). How to meditate. Mindful; Mindful Communications & Such PBC. https://www.mindful.org/how-to-meditate/

Selenite meaning: Healing Properties & everyday uses. (n.d.). Tiny Rituals. https://tinyrituals.co/blogs/tiny-rituals/selenite-meaning-healing-properties-everyday-uses

Short, E. (2021, November 10). 7 signs of negative energy in a person. Mål Paper. https://malpaper.com/blogs/news/7-signs-of-negative-energy-in-a-person

Signs of negative energy. (n.d.). WebMD. https://www.webmd.com/balance/signs-negative-energy

Son, N. T. (2023, March 14). 20 how many crystals are there? Advanced Guide 07/2023. Soccercentralph. https://thcsnguyenthanhson.edu.vn/20-how-many-crystals-are-there-advanced-guide/

Spiritual illnesses. (n.d.). Stanford.edu. https://geriatrics.stanford.edu/ethnomed/hmong/fund/spiritual_illnesses.html

Stelter, G. (2016, October 4). Chakras: A beginner's guide to the 7 chakras. Healthline. https://www.healthline.com/health/fitness-exercise/7-chakras

StMU. (2021, September 27). Sweet Grass. StMU; St. Mary's University. https://stmu.ca/sweet-grass/

The College of Psychic Studies : Enlighten : What is a psychic attack. (n.d.). The College of Psychic Studies. https://www.collegeofpsychicstudies.co.uk/enlighten/what-is-a-psychic-attack/

The complete guide to smudging. (n.d.). JL Local. https://jllocal.com/blogs/articles/2

The Sacred Art of Smudging. (n.d.). Kripalu. https://kripalu.org/resources/sacred-art-smudging

Theodora Blanchfield, A. (2022, January 31). How to meditate with crystals. Verywell Mind. https://www.verywellmind.com/how-to-meditate-with-crystals-5214020

TIMESOFINDIA.COM. (2020, September 12). How to identify negative energies at your home and remove them. Times Of India. https://timesofindia.indiatimes.com/life-style/home-garden/how-to-identify-negative-energies-at-your-home-and-remove-them/articleshow/78075353.cms

UPLIFT. (2017, August 8). The science behind smudging. UPLIFT. https://uplift.love/the-science-behind-smudging/

Ward, K. (2021, December 14). How to program a crystal with your intention, because yes, you should be doing that. Yahoo Sports. https://sports.yahoo.com/program-crystal-intention-because-yes-173400639.html

What Is Shamanic Smudging? (n.d.). Incensewarehouse.Com. https://www.incensewarehouse.com/What-Is-Shamanic-Smudging_ep_30-1.html

White, A. (2018, July 18). 10 benefits of burning sage, how to get started, and more. Healthline. https://www.healthline.com/health/benefits-of-burning-sage

Williams, R. (2018, July 17). Enhance your meditation practice with crystals. Chopra. https://chopra.com/articles/enhance-your-meditation-practice-with-crystals

Willis, K. K. (2016, January 18). Grief and rage: The connection between 4th and 1st chakras. Lucid Body | Acting Classes and Coaching for the Physical Actor. https://lucidbody.com/blog/grief-and-rage-the-connection-between-4th-and-1st-chakras/

www.ingramcontent.com/pod-product-compliance
Lightning Source LLC
Chambersburg PA
CBHW051848160426
43209CB00006B/1208